THE
OUTPLACEMENT
SOLUTION

THE
OUTPLACEMENT
SOLUTION

Getting the Right Job
After Mergers, Takeovers, Layoffs,
and Other Corporate Chaos

KAREN WOLFER

RICHARD G. WONG

WILEY

John Wiley & Sons, Inc.
New York • Chichester • Brisbane • Toronto • Singapore

Publisher: Stephen Kippur
Editor: Katherine Schowalter
Managing Editor: Corinne McCormick

Library of Congress Cataloging-in-Publication Data

Wolfer, Karen.
      The outplacement solution: getting the right job after mergers, takeovers, layoffs, and other corporate chaos.

      Bibliography: p.
      1. Vocational guidance.   2. Job hunting   3. Career.
changes.   I. Wong, Richard G.   II. Title.
HF5381.W79   1988   650.1'4   87-17325
ISBN 0-471-62083-1 (pbk.)

Printed in the United States of America
88 89 10 9 8 7 6 5 4 3 2 1

To my spouse, Fredric
—KW

To my children Scott and Nicole Wong.
—RW

Acknowledgments

We wish to extend our appreciation to Helen Hayes for her initial encouragement in putting this book together; Stephanie Culp for hand carrying our manuscript to our publisher; John Jones and Barbara Beckman for editorial assistance.

Contents

Foreword

At a recent conference I asked an audience of six hundred personnel professionals for a show of hands from those representing organizations that either recently have undergone "downsizing" or were about to initiate that activity. Over 95 percent raised their hands! This phenomenon is, of course, unsettling—both to the organization and particularly to the individuals who are "let go." They may be "outplaced," "laid off," "dismissed," "stimulated" into early retirement, or put on a kind of "taxi squad," as some professional football players are. However you call it, being let go is a compelling experience. You have to do something about it if it affects you.

Karen Wolfer and Rich Wong have laid out a step-by-step method for picking up the pieces, assessing yourself, developing an action plan, and getting on with the business of finding a suitable next position. Their advice is sound and practical. A word of caution, however. Research indicates that only a small minority of persons like yourself actually go all of the way through a book like this. They tend to work on several exercises, begin to feel better, and then lay the project aside. In your case, that could be disastrous. Do the entire program.

The developers of this system are highly qualified to help you make your transition from being let go to entering a new position that is "right" for you. Both have worked with hundreds of people affected by economic difficulties within organizations. Both have developed programs to assist employees to find ways of expressing themselves through work in another setting. They actively consult with companies that are contemplating downsizing. They know what it takes to get through the upsetting experience of leaving one job and finding another. Their best judgments about what works are included in these pages. If you want to reestablish your self-esteem and find a path for yourself, go through the whole program. As Noel Coward once said, when the conditions are right, "Work is more fun than fun."

John E. Jones
Human Relations Consultant
San Diego, California

Introduction

There are many excellent self-help books already on the book shelves aimed at helping people obtain a job. This workbook is unique in that it addresses a new phenomenon in today's fast-paced world of mergers, reorganizations, divestments, relocations, and layoffs. It deals with the emotional trauma of faithful, competent, long-term employees who joined large institutions such as AT&T and Bank of America with the expectation that, in exchange for their loyalty and dedication, they would have the security of a job until retirement. Dramatic sweeping economic conditions have forced these and other companies to reevaluate their earlier traditions of long-term, permanent employment, with devastating personal results. It is estimated that approximately 400,000 middle managers will be laid off by 1990.[1]

We originally wrote this book as a companion work for a workshop on handling the transition from being let go through the successful reestablishing of oneself in a new position. Due to many requests we are making this book available individually.

PART 1

Taking Good Care of Yourself

If you are reading this book, you have probably recently been "let go" from your job. In many cases you have devoted more time to the organization you are leaving than to any other relationship, including school, the service, or your family. Some of the feelings you probably are experiencing—shock, anger, disbelief, injustice, hopelessness, loss—are normal and facing them is the first step in starting your new life. The loss of a job creates an emotional wound. When an emotional injury has taken place, the body begins a process of healing. Let the process happen—trust it. Know the emotional hurt will pass, and when it passes you will be a stronger, happier, and more aware person.

The purpose of this section is to work with you through the grief stage of leaving an organization where you have spent a considerable amount of time and energy and to help formulate the next stage of your life. Grieving follows three stages: shock/denial, anger/depression, and understanding/ acceptance. Progression through these stages occurs with any type of loss. The only difference is the length of time it takes to go through the three stages and the intensity of emotion felt during each. The following series of worksheets is designed to aid in this process and to help you focus on what your options for the future are.

Your Present State of Mind

Below are emotions. You may be feeling many of these or just a few. We will repeat this exercise again in the workbook, so you may want to date this chart to allow you, at a later date, to see how well you are recovering.

INSTRUCTIONS:

Check (√) which of the following words describe your present state of mind:

___ Anger	___ Tearful	___ Grumpy
___ Bitter	___ What's next?	___ Heroic
___ Outrage	___ Finality	___ Hideous
___ Hurt	___ Tight chested	___ Horrible
___ Shock	___ Freedom	___ Ignorant
___ Disbelief	___ Fright	___ Imbecile
___ Anxiety	___ Autonomous	___ Inactive
___ Depressed	___ Argumentative	___ Incapacitated
___ Self-doubt	___ Apprehensive	___ Incisive
___ Humiliation	___ Ambiguous	___ Inspired
___ Shame	___ Abnormal	___ Jovial
___ Fear	___ Detached	___ Lavish
___ Relief	___ Docile	___ Lonesome
___ Conclusion	___ Dogmatic	___ Lovable
___ Beaten	___ Elation	___ Malicious
___ Loser	___ Endless	___ Moody
___ Whole	___ Feeble	___ Obsolete
___ Confusion	___ Forgiving	___ Paranoia

_____ Chaotic	_____ Free	_____ Perplexed
_____ Comatose	_____ Frolic	_____ Rejuvenated
_____ Calm	_____ Futile	_____ Scapegoat
_____ Cohesive	_____ Strong	

_____ Other _____

          (Specify)

What does losing a job feel like? The obvious feelings of pain, depression and/or sadness are all possible reactions. Other possible reactions are:

- feeling helpless, fearful, empty, despairing, negative, irritable, angry, guilty, restless;
- loss of concentration, motivation, hope, or energy;
- changes in appetite, sexual drives, or sleep patterns;
- tendency to be tired and accident-prone.

Any or all of these can be expected during and after the experience of losing your job.

The first stage of grieving is shock/denial. Some words that describe this stage are:

Confusion, Chaotic, Comatose, What's next?, Apprehensive, Ambiguous, Detached, Docile, Endless, Feeble, Perplexed, Ignorant, Imbecile, Inactive, Incapacitated, Obsolete, Scapegoat, Shock and Disbelief.

The second stage of grieving is anger/depression. Some words that describe this stage are:

Anxiety, Self-doubt, Fear, Tight-chested, Abnormal, Paranoia, Hurt, Depression, Beaten, Tearful, Lonesome, Anger, Bitterness, Outrage, Humiliation, Shame, Loser, Argumentative, Dogmatic, Futile, Grumpy, Hideous, Horrible, Malicious, Moody.

The third stage of grieving is understanding/acceptance. Some words that describe this stage are:

> Relief, Conclusion, Whole, Calm, Cohesive, Finality, Freedom, Autonomous, Elation, Forgiving, Free, Frolic, Heroic, Incisive, Inspired, Jovial, Lavish, Lovable, Rejuvenated, Strong.

Take a look at the items you checked (√). Do you see a pattern? Are the words you checked in one stage more than another? Or do you have equal amount of checks in all three stages?

The grieving process is different for each person. The important issue is to know where you are within the process. After you have reached stage three, your outlook on life will become positive and allow you to project a positive self-image during your job search. No employer wants a sad-sack, hostile "victim" for an employee.

You can expect to be in shock for a while. You may struggle both to believe and to disbelieve that this is happening to you. It is important that you feel the hurt. Don't deny it or cover it or run away from it. If you're angry, it's okay, but let the anger out. Hit a pillow, kick, scream, yell, play volleyball, handball, tennis, play a musical instrument as loud and aggressively as you can. If anger is channeled into harmless or constructive ways, you'll avoid senseless arguments, accidents, possible ulcers, and maybe even create something positive.

If you find that none of these words describe your current frame of mind, and are more positive; then good for you! You are on the right track.

Priorities

When things are not going your way, you feel as if you're spinning your wheels, lost, or hopeless ... it may be time to take a look at what's important to you. Establishing priorities help you focus on what's important to you. Priorities provide order, a sense of accomplishment, direction, and purpose to your life. This is especially important at a time when you have lost your job—lost the activity that fulfilled many of these needs. It may be necessary to readjust your priorities and/or activities. You may even find that your focus is on your top priorities but you are unrealistic about the amount of time to achieve your plans.

INSTRUCTIONS:

Rank the following in order of importance to you. Write a "1" in front of the most important, a "2" next, and so on.

_____ Affection

_____ Duty

_____ Finding a job

_____ Leadership

_____ Parenthood

_____ Physical fitness

_____ Power

_____ Providing basic for family/self

_____ Security

_____ Self-realization

_____ Status Quo

_____ Control

_____ Experience

_____ Independence

_____ Learning

_____ Personal relationships

_____ Pleasure

_____ Prestige

_____ Risk-taking

_____ Self-image

_____ Service

_____ Wealth

Take a look at your top five priorities. Ask yourself the following questions:

- Where am I spending my time?

- What have I done today/this week to meet my top priorities?

- How much time have I devoted to accomplishing my top priorities versus others?

If you are not happy about how you are spending your time, or if you notice that your daily/weekly activities do not help you achieve your top-priority items, then you need to either change your priorities or change activities. At this point in your life you have experienced a lot of anger, hurt, and frustration. There is no need to create more with unrealistic or unclear goals/priorities.

Some tips to achieve your priorities:

- Create a things-to-do list every day, at the same time each day.
- Review each item and determine high, low, or no value in meeting your priority issues.
- Star each item that has high value.
- Allocate a specified amount of time to accomplish each starred item.
- Schedule when you will do the starred items.
- Do high-value starred items first.
- If all high-value starred items are not completed that day, carry over to next day and reprioritize again (yesterday's highs may be today's lows).

There are no right or wrong priorities, and you can expect your priorities to shift as you progress through your job search. When you are experiencing emotional hurt, it is easy to lose focus on what's important to you. You may even find yourself just reacting to life and situations without any purposeful action. This often happens when you are in stage one of grieving—shock/denial. Being able to focus large parts of your time and efforts on your top priorities is a sign that you are entering stage three—understanding/acceptance.

Regardless of your priorities it is important to maintain or develop (as the case may be) good nutritional habits. Now is not the time to alter your eating habits by going on a crash diet. But decrease junk food, and "calorie junkies" beware! You may tend to overeat during this time, and unwanted inches may cause a lower self-image, resulting in more depression.

Personal Heroes/Heroines

INSTRUCTIONS:

Identify your personal heroes and/or heroines; list their qualities and/or characteristics:

Name	Name

Qualities and/or Characteristics	Qualities and/or Characteristics

_____	_____
_____	_____
_____	_____
_____	_____
Name	Name

Qualities and/or Character-istics

Qualities and/or Character-istics

Are there common qualities among your heroes/heroines?

Are they positive or negative?

Do you have these qualities?

Do people around you have these qualities?

It's nice to have a hero, someone who stands out—"The Good Guy." Being able to identify what makes you admire someone helps you find these qualities in other relationships. It also makes you feel good. Reading about a hero is a positive feeling. Start expecting a positive outcome. Anticipate it. Plan for it. It will come. There is great power in a positive attitude.

Vision

A vision provides you with long-term direction. It sets tone and direction to your life. In other words, what are your dreams.

INSTRUCTIONS:

In a few sentences, write about what your life mission is— your vision of the ideal life situation for you.

Why is this important to you?

The key thoughts are change and opportunity. Prepare to make an adjustment ... maybe two or even three. A new chapter in your life has begun. Now is the time to remold your life toward the ideal. It's a time to realize opportunity. It will take courage, but at the same time it's exciting. This might turn out to be fun.

The following questions will help you formulate a plan to achieve your vision.

1. I wish to change or improve:

2. The outcome I want is:

3. My target date is:

4. Action items/activities to help me accomplish my vision are:

5. List the action items/activities that are the most important:

6. List the key people to be involved:

7. I will know I have been successful when:

Go back to the priority exercise and check to see that the action items/activities is where you are spending your time. To accomplish your vision it must become a priority.

Aspirations

An aspiration is similar to a vision because it provides direction to your life. An aspiration, however, is narrower in focus. Aspirations deal more with ambition and eagerness for advancement, honor, recognition, and so on. It's the longing, craving, the hope for power, importance, and excellence.

INSTRUCTIONS:

In a few sentences, answer the following questions.

What do you want to do that you're not doing?

What intrigues you?

What haven't you done in a long time?

What were your dreams when you finished school?

Review your answers. Are these the things that make you happy? If so, there should be some relationship between your vision and priorities. Go back and check.

Remember, now is the time to make new friends, associates, colleagues. Attend meetings, concerts, plays, socials—any public gathering. Meet your neighbors. Read a book. Take a class. Learn—and above all, do something new or something that lets you experience the thrill and eagerness of being alive.

Favorite Quotes

Interspersed throughout this workbook are our favorite quotations. You are encouraged to write in your own. Often these "wise words" have a strong motivational effect, and can be useful to review when you have had "one of those days."

"The mass of men live lives of quiet desperation."
Henry David Thoreau, *Walden*[2]

Use the space below to write your favorite quotes.

Accomplishments/ Achievements

You have been through a lot. During stage one of the grieving process, shock/denial, accomplishments and achievements vanish. While in stage two, anger/depression, you remember some accomplishments and achievements but usually in a hostile negative way. In stage three, understanding and acceptance, you are ready to move on, to let go of the past, to rebuild and form a future. A step in that direction is to remember and hang on to your past accomplishments and achievements.

This exercise will help you in two ways. First it helps rebuild your own self-worth and builds self-confidence. Second, many people have difficulty giving themselves a pat on the back. This will help you learn how to talk about yourself in a positive and meaningful way. This will be useful during the interview process.

INSTRUCTIONS:
Find a quiet place and take a few moments to reflect on the things you have done that you are proud of. It might be something in your professional life or perhaps an occurrence in your personal life.

Now think about why these things were important to you —made you proud of yourself. Remember, accomplishments are relative and judged in a very personal manner, only by you.

In the space below, describe at least five of your accomplishments and add some notes about why it was important to _you_.

1.

2.

3.

4.

5.

Your self-esteem may have suffered a jolt, and your thoughts may be full of guilt, worry, and condemnation. These thoughts are just symptoms of the stress you are going through. There is no need to give negative thoughts about yourself prime-time status. So let's focus on things you can be proud of—things that remind you that you're worthwhile.

Skills Analysis

Once the hurt is less, understanding can grow, and you will be entering the third stage—understanding/acceptance. The relationship you had with your previous employer brought you a great deal of good (that's why you missed it so terribly when it was no longer there). Much of it is still with you, and now is the time to take stock of that good. That job taught you a great deal of many things. It's important that you be able to talk about your skills and previous employment easily. You need to know what your skills are in very specific terms. Many people can't describe their skills "off the top of their heads," so a skills analysis is necessary. This exercise will take you through the steps involved in a skills analysis.

WHAT IS A SKILL?

What employers mean when they talk about skills is:

1. *Things you can do.* Employers want to know the specific actions you can do, such as "operate equipment," "ability to proofread," or "organize an effective presentation."

2. *Working conditions and roles.* Employers want to know how well you fit into the workplace, and if you will get along with the other employees. Are you used to working in an office or outdoors? Are you outgoing and friendly, or quiet and keep to yourself?

3. *Things you know.* Jobs require knowledge and skill. Employers want to know if you know the basics of the job.

A step-by-step approach will help you get a complete and useful picture of your skills. The first step is to list all the jobs you have done.

16

Use the SKILLS-ANALYSIS WORKSHEET, on the next page, to do your analysis. Start by listing each job you have had at the top of each SKILLS-ANALYSIS WORKSHEET. If you have held different jobs within the same company, fill out a separate SKILLS-ANALYSIS WORKSHEET for each job.

Now for each job consider all three categories—Things You Can Do, Working Conditions and Roles, and Things You Know. Each of these categories is explained in detail, and steps are provided to help you complete the worksheet.

Skills-analysis Worksheet

Job: _____

Things I Can Do

Working Conditions

Things I Know

Skills-analysis Worksheet

Job: _____

Things I Can Do

Working Conditions

Things I Know

Skills-analysis Worksheet

Job: _____

Things I Can Do

Working Conditions

Things I Know

Skills-analysis Worksheet

Job: _____

Things I Can Do

Working Conditions

Things I Know

Skills-analysis Worksheet

Job: _____

Things I Can Do

Working Conditions

Things I Know

Skills-analysis Worksheet

Job: _____

Things I Can Do

Working Conditions

Things I Know

Skills-analysis Worksheet

Job: _____

Things I Can Do

Working Conditions

Things I Know

Skills-analysis Worksheet

Job: _____

Things I Can Do

Working Conditions

Things I Know

Skills-analysis Worksheet

Job: _____

Things I Can Do

Working Conditions

Things I Know

Skills-analysis Worksheet

Job: _____

Things I Can Do

Working Conditions

Things I Know

THINGS YOU CAN DO

This first step is to list specific actions, not the general ones we usually use to describe our work. If your job was "manager," don't list your skill as "managing people."

Instead, try to list the things you did to "manage"—organized people, made decisions, scheduled work, conducted performance reviews, developed budgets, and so on. It's these specific skills that are the key to finding another job.

Here are some examples:

> Quality Control Engineer—I inspected finished products for conformity to standards. I reviewed production techniques. Communicated quality standards to vendors, selected supply vendors and monitored their products. Designed statistical sampling technique, inspected materials used in manufacturing, recommended improvements, wrote quality production reports, and so on.

> Finance Manager—I prepared a monthly budget, advised executive board on cash-flow requirements weekly, disbursed funds, bought supplies, made suggestions for improved budget procedures, implemented pro forma computer package, participated in executive meetings, and so on.

If you are still having some problems making a complete list, try the following ideas:

Think about what you did with things, information, and people. Thinking about a job in these terms may help jog your mind. For example, if you were a waiter the list would look something like this:

Working with things: I sorted silverware, organized the tables in the room, maintained the job list in the kitchen, organized the fountain area, logged and issued order checks daily, operated computerized cash register.

Working with information: I interpreted directions, organized instructions, kept accurate records, memorized orders and names quickly, memorized daily specials and garnish requirements.

Working with people: I helped them make decisions, gave advice, made them feel at ease, established a friendly relationship quickly, sold the items, anticipated their needs, followed up with each order.

If you're still finding it hard to think about your skills, use the checklist below.

SKILLS CHECKLIST

Have you ever done any of these?

Advised	Built	Danced
Adapted	Budgeted	Defined
Administered	Calculated	Delivered
Alphabetized	Checked	Delegated
Analyzed	Communicated	Demonstrated
Arranged	Compared	Described
Arbitrated	Conducted	Designed
Assembled	Counseled	Decorated
Articulated	Controlled	Developed
Assigned	Consulted	Directed
Assisted	Coordinated	Documented
Audited	Collaborated	Drove
Automated	Clarified	Enforced
Bought	Critiqued	Empathized

Established	Lubricated	Represented
Evaluated	Maintained	Scheduled
Examined	Marketed	Served
Expanded	Measured	Shipped
Expressed	Memorized	Solved
Forecast	Mixed	Sorted
Formulated	Moderated	Summarized
Guided	Modeled	Stocked
Hired	Monitored	Spoke
Implemented	Negotiated	Sold
Improved	Observed	Tabulated
Informed	Operated	Tested
Influenced	Organized	Translated
Initiated	Planned	Trained
Inspected	Prepared	Trimmed
Inspired	Programmed	Trouble Shot
Interviewed	Proposed	Typed
Judged	Polished	Unloaded
Justified	Recorded	Washed
Labeled	Routed	Wrote
Lectured	Repaired	Weighed
Listened	Recommended	

Now complete the "Things I Can Do" section of your SKILLS-ANALYSIS WORKSHEETS.

WORKING CONDITIONS

The purpose of this part of the skills analysis is to think about what working conditions and roles you can handle. There are no right sets of working conditions and roles; different employers want different kinds of people. The key to success is matching yourself to the employer, finding an employer who wants someone just like you.

Working conditions are both physical and psychological. They include things like temperature, work pace, amount of stress, type of work space, and competition. Since you are starting over, let's look for a job that is tailored to your likes.

For help to get started in thinking about working conditions and roles, complete the next two checklists.

WORKING-CONDITIONS CHECKLIST

INSTRUCTIONS:

Place a (√) check on items you can handle or adapt to:

Physical Conditions

_____ Heavy labor	_____ Office with windows
_____ Travel	_____ Own office
_____ Stand all day	_____ Work in open office
_____ Precise machine work	_____ Must wear uniform
_____ Lift heavy objects	_____ Strict dress code
_____ Outdoor work	_____ No dress code
_____ Indoor work	_____ Air conditioned
_____ Drive	_____ Assigned Parking
_____ Temperature extremes	_____ Parking provided
_____ Physical risks (fire, etc.)	_____ Sit all day
_____ Odd work hours	_____ Uses computer
_____ High places	_____ Smoking or non-smoking

_____ Read a lot   _____ Noisy conditions

_____ Write a lot   _____ Crowded conditions

_____ Operate a variety of   _____ Other
      equipment

      Work around hazard-
_____ ous chemicals

Psychological Conditions

_____ Live near work   _____ Work by yourself

_____ Stay in same job for   _____ Take orders
      years
                                    _____ Work under stress
_____ Work on-call
                                    _____ Many different kinds
_____ Work with elderly   of work

_____ Work with young   _____ Work steady hours
      adults
                                    _____ Make decisions
_____ Make your own hours
                                    _____ Work with other
_____ Express your opinions   people
      freely
                                    _____ Move often
_____ Repetitive work
                                    _____ Work in large
_____ Work to full ability   company

_____ Work as a team   _____ Work in small office,
      member   town

_____ Work independently   _____ Political work

_____ Creative work   _____ Overtime work

_____ Work under deadlines   _____ Public contact

_____ Work odd hours

_____ Compete with others

_____ Plan and schedule your own work

_____ Work with individuals

_____ Work with college students

_____ Work with teenagers

_____ Other

_____ Do only part of a job

_____ Move up fast

_____ Do same job every day

_____ Work with babies

_____ Work with school-age children

_____ Work with people of all ages

_____ Work on commission

Go over your list and circle those items you're willing to handle in a new job.

WORKING-ROLES CHECKLIST

INSTRUCTIONS:

Some common roles are listed here. Jot down notes about your experience within each of these roles.

1. Have you ever been in charge of a project? _____

_____

2. Have you worked on a team to get a job done? _____

_____

3. Have you ever been a trainer? _____

4. Have you ever supervised or given direction to others?

_____

5. Have you ever carried out instructions? _____

_____

6. Have you ever made major decisions on your job? ___

_____

7. Have you ever negotiated a contract? _____

_____

8. Have you ever solved a labor dispute? _____

_____

9. Have you ever had to sell an idea? _____

_____

10. Have you ever coordinated an activity for someone?

_____

11. Have you ever reviewed large amounts of material and
extracted its essence? _____

_____

12. Have you ever dealt with numbers, performing simple
or complex arithmetic? _____

_____

13. Have you ever organized people to get a job done? ___

_____

14. Have you ever done preventative work? _____

_____

15. Have you ever operated a computer? _____

_____

16. Have you ever monitored, adjusted, or serviced auto-

matic machines while they were running? _____

_____

17. Have you ever handled a variety of tasks simultan-
    eously? _____

18. Have you ever systematically accomplished tasks? ___

    _____

19. Have you ever brought order out of chaos? _____

    _____

20. Have you ever recognized obsolescence of ideas or pro-
    cedures before verifiable data were available? _____

    _____

Use the answers from these two checklists to complete the
"Working Conditions" section of your SKILLS-ANALYSIS
WORKSHEETS.

THINGS YOU KNOW

Specific jobs require specific kinds of knowledge, creden-
tials, and degrees. Many jobs will be open on the basis of
what is called "equivalent experience." What you must be
able to do is to convince the employer that you are qualified
on the basis of your other work experience, even though
you may have never had that actual type of job before. Even
if you have had no "formal training" you probably know a
lot about more subjects than you think. You have learned
from experience, from working with other people.
The key to dealing with "equivalent experience" is to remember you are not your job title. Stop thinking of yourself
as a "Bookkeeper," "Teacher," or "Systems Analyst." Remove those titles from your vocabulary. When you talk to
your friends, relatives, or peers, how would they describe

you? If it's with a job title (Salesperson, EDP Auditor, Manager) then it's time for you to start thinking and talking about your skills and knowledge. This is a very important step if you are trying to change careers or work in a different industry.

Before you finalize the third part of the SKILLS-ANALYSIS WORKSHEET, review the following list of examples of knowledge skills.

Work Experience *In your work, if you have:*	General Knowledge *Then you probably know:*
Written company letters	Business-writing formats
Kept time sheets and payroll information	IRS reporting requirements
Established friendly relationships quickly	Interpersonal skills
Delivered funds to the bank	Bank security procedures
Filed a complaint against a supervisor	Employee-relations law (some)
Purchased office supplies	Quantity purchasing requirements
Operated precision machinery	Safety rules
Inspected a company product	Basic quality-control procedures
Raised money for nonprofit company	Fund-raising techniques
Kept a set of books	Basic accounting principles
Hired and terminated employees	Personnel policies (some)

Repaired a complicated machine	Trouble-shooting principles
Wrote computer programs	Systematic analysis
Trained someone to take your job	How people learn

Remember, you want to be able to talk about your skill and knowledge—not job titles—to prospective employers. So as you analyze each of your jobs, start by naming your experience, and then name the knowledge you needed to do these things.

Now complete the "Things I Know" Section of your SKILLS-ANALYSIS WORKSHEETS.

Making a Skills Matrix

After you have completed the SKILLS-ANALYSIS WORK-SHEET, stop, take a break, and treat yourself to something special. You have completed a very difficult task. When you're ready, the next step is making a skills matrix.

You may ask, why am I doing this? This step enables you to tell an employer convincingly what your strengths are, and in what order of priority. This step helps avoid "wishy-washy" answers in the interview.

I know, some of you may be thinking, "I already know what my skills and knowledge are and they are all in the wrong field." This process will force you to look for the crossover skills that will apply to a new industry or career and prior-itize them in order of importance to you. This then becomes the first step in identifying what skill areas you need to increase your proficiency.

First sum up your skills into a matrix about yourself. To make a skills matrix, you first scan your SKILLS-ANALYSIS WORKSHEET and look for repeat skills. Suppose, for example, that you find you have trained other people in six of eight jobs you have held. This is obviously a major skill area, something you might think of as a strength and an area where you may have great proficiency.

Across the top, list your skills in descending order according to how well you honestly believe you *perform* the skills. Then list your skills down the left-hand column according to how much you honestly *enjoy* performing the skills. Then darken the boxes where the skills coincide.

PERFORMANCE

		1	2	3	4	5	6	7	8	Low
	Do Best									
Enjoy Most	High 1									
E	2									
N	3									
J										
O	4									
Y	5									
M										
E	6									
N	7									
T	8									
	Low									

Darkened boxes in upper left represent the skills that you are the best at and enjoy the most.

GROUPING YOUR SKILLS

The skills matrix helps you identify what skills you enjoy and perform well. It will also help you explain your skills to an employer. A skills grouping will help you identify the kinds of employers and jobs you should look for.

Different jobs require different groups of skills. For example, a salesperson primarily needs "Selling" skills, "Service" skills, and some "Management" skills. A teacher doesn't need a lot of "Manual" skills or "Agricultural" skills. If by some chance you wanted to be a salesperson, you would look at your skills to see how many of the "Selling" skills you have.

Another way to use job grouping is to locate the grouping area you like the best and see how many of these skills you have. This will help you identify what skills you need to develop.

Skills groups on the next page can give you clues to the types of jobs for which employers would probably like to hire you. These skills categories are commonly used by career counselors.

Review each group and place a check mark ($\sqrt{}$) at each skill you have. Then count each check mark under each grouping and write the number in the appropriate space on the GROUPING-YOUR-SKILLS WORKSHEET. Review the results to see where you have the most skills. For example, if you look at your skills list and find that you have:

    12 Communication Skills
     9 Management Skills
     8 Financial Skills
     4 Manual Skills
     3 Service Skills
     2 Research Skills

Then look for jobs that emphasize the Communication, Management, and Financial skills. The point in job grouping is not to put yourself into a box but to see where your strengths are. You will notice that some skills are in more than one place because there is overlap. If some of your skills are not listed, write them in where you feel they best fit.

JOB GROUPINGS[3]

CLERICAL SKILLS
Examining
Evaluating
Filing
Developing methods
Improving
Recording
Computing
Recommending
Work as team member
Work in office
Do routine office work
Basic clerical skills
Bookkeeping
Data-entry operations
Telephone protocol

AGRICULTURAL SKILLS
Diagnosing malfunctions
Repairing engines
Maintaining machinery
Packing
Replacing defective parts
Woodworking
Constructing building
Hitching

Work outdoors
Work in varied climate
Manual work
Do heavy work
Operating basic machinery
Safety rules
Welding
Horticultural procedures

FINANCIAL SKILLS
Calculating
Projecting
Budgeting
Recognize problems
Solve problems
Finger dexterity
Able to concentrate
Handle detail work
Work under stress
Orderly thinking
Accounting procedures
Data processing
Operate business
    machines
Financial concepts
Investment principles

TECHNICAL SKILLS
Financing
Evaluating
Calculating
Adjusting controls
Aligning fixtures
Following specifications
Observing indicators
Verifying
Drafting
Work in an office/outdoors
Work in small studios
Odd hours
Economics
Investigation principles

MANAGEMENT SKILLS
Planning
Organizing
Scheduling
Assigning/Delegating
Directing
Hiring
Measuring production
Selling standards
Work under stress
Work with people
Travel frequently
Work as a team member
Personnel practices
Time management
Negotiating strategies

SELLING SKILLS
Contacting
Persuading
Reviewing products

Inspecting products
Determining value
Informing buyers
Promoting sales
Work outdoors/indoors
Work with people
Work under stress
Work long hours
Knowledge of products
Human relations
Financing
Budgeting

COMMUNICATION SKILLS
Reasoning
Organizing
Defining
Writing
Listening
Explaining
Interpreting ideas
Reading
Handle precise work
Work with committees
Public speaking
Correct English usage
Subject knowledge
Operate communication
    systems
Good sense of timing

MANUAL SKILLS
Operating
Monitoring
Controlling
Setting-up
Driving
Cutting

Do precise machine work
Do heavy work
Work on assembly line
Work independently
Knowledge of tools
Safety rules
Basic mechanics
Basic plumbing
Electronic principles

PUBLIC RELATIONS
Planning
Conducting
Maintaining favorable image
Informing the public
Consulting
Write news release
Researching
Work with people
Work under stress
Work very long hours
Negotiating principles
Media process
Human relations

MAINTENANCE SKILLS
Repairing equipment
Maintaining equipment
Operating tools
Dismantling
Removing parts
Adjusting functional parts
Lubricating/cleaning parts
Purchasing/ordering parts
Climbing
Work indoors/outdoors
Lift heavy equipment

Work as a team member
Basic mechanics
Electrical principles
Plumbing principles

RESEARCH SKILLS
Recognizing problems
Interviewing
Developing questions
Synthesizing
Writing
Diagnosing
Collecting data
Extrapolating
Reviewing
Work with direction
Work very long hours
Work on long-term projects
Statistics
Algebra
Research design

SERVICE SKILLS
Counseling
Guiding
Leading
Listening
Coordinating
Work under stress
Respond to emergencies
Work under hazardous
  conditions
Work on weekends
Work night shifts
Knowledge of a subject
Human-behavior principles
Community resources

Grouping-your-skills Worksheet

INSTRUCTIONS:

Place the total number of ($\checkmark$) marks under each Job-Grouping Category below.

_____ Clerical Skills

_____ Agricultural Skills

_____ Management Skills

_____ Financial Skills

_____ Technical Skills

_____ Selling Skills

_____ Communication Skills

_____ Manual Skills

_____ Public Relations Skills

_____ Maintenance Skills

_____ Research Skills

_____ Service Skills

The top three skill groupings represent the types of jobs for which employers would probably like to hire you.

"Sometimes you can't admit you're scared. You just keep going until you get it right."
Ralph Ward, _Forbes_[4]

Personal Journal

The next few weeks or months are going to require a maximum amount of effort, discipline, and dedication on your part. In addition, you can anticipate feeling at times, discouragement, abandonment, and/or self-pity. You are strongly encouraged to write a few lines at the end of each day on your activities and mental state. Remember this is the time to pamper yourself: redecorate, or at least clean out your house closet or garage; buy or make something new; go back to college and learn whatever it is you've always wanted to know; take a long uninterrupted shower; read a good book; take a nap; visit a long-lost friend; go for a walk. The list is endless. Use the next few pages to start your journal, then simply buy a notebook and continue using the technique.

Date: _____

What have I accomplished today?

What do I feel about myself today?

What did I do today as a special treat to myself?

Personal Journal

Date: _____

What I've accomplished today?

What I feel about myself today?

What did I do today as a special treat to myself?

Personal Journal

Date: _____

What I've accomplished today?

What I feel about myself today?

What did I do today as a special treat to myself?

PART 2

Keeping an Eye on Finances

Keeping an Eye on
Finances

Finances

The best advice we'll give you is to start immediately and actively seeking your next job, to assess your present financial position, and to take steps to cut back on all but the barest necessities. To help you look at your financial situation realistically, fill out the following.

Date: _____

- **Nest Egg**

  Severance Pay $ _____

  Savings   _____

  Retirement Accounts   _____

  Other _____   _____

- **Monthly Income**

  Unemployment Insurance   _____

  Spouse's Salary   _____

  Rental Income   _____

  Other _____   _____
      (Specify)
               TOTAL $ _____

- **Monthly Expenses**

  Rent/Mortgage $ _____

  Automobile   _____

  Insurance   _____

  Utilities   _____

  Food   _____

  Clothing   _____

Medical/Dental   _____

Recreation   _____

Credit Card Payments   _____

Alimony or Child Support   _____

Day Care   _____

Other _____   _____
        (Specify)

               TOTAL $ _____

Now add a 15 percent increase to monthly expenses. We have found that many people are overly optimistic.

Is there a positive or negative difference between Monthly Income and Monthly Expenses?

If you happen to have a positive balance, celebrate! However, it may still be necessary to review where cutbacks could occur, as a backup position, if your status remains unemployed for a lengthy period of time.

If you have a negative balance, take action now to protect your assets and credit rating. Mortgage companies, banks and credit card companies will often work with you to reduce monthly payments for a period of time. Creditors would much rather hear from you first than them having to contact you. Many communities have free financial counseling as part of the Social Services Department. If you feel you still need additional help, we recommend the book *"The RIF Survival Handbook: How to Manage Your Money if You're Unemployed,"* by John May (Tilden Press, 1737 DeSales St. NW, Ste. 300, Washington, DC 20036).

Unemployment Insurance

Over the years your employer has paid 1 percent (or more) of your salary for unemployment insurance. You are entitled to it.

1. Apply immediately: File your claim after your final day of work. DO NOT WAIT. Generally speaking, you are only eligible for six months of unemployment insurance, so if you don't apply immediately and get a job before the end of the six-month period, you lose those payments.

2. Where to apply: Look in the white pages of your local telephone directory under State Governmental Offices. Look for one of the following: Employment Development Department, Employee Assistance or Unemployment Insurance Claims. Call the office nearest your home and find out the office hours and if you can make an appointment to file your unemployment insurance claim.

3. To apply, bring with you the following information:
- Pen
- Social Security Number
- Previous employer's name, address, and position held for the last three years
- Reason for leaving previous employers
—Be truthful in explaining the reason you were let go. The interviewer will verify your reason with your former employer.

4. Tax Reform Act of 1986: Beginning in 1986, all unemployment compensation benefits that you receive are to be included in your annual taxable gross income (Stephen J. Shay CPA, Shay & Associates, Laguna Hills, CA. 92653). Make sure you keep records of all payments received.

5. General tips:
- Be on time for your appointment.
- Dress in your normal business attire.

—It will help you maintain a positive self-image. Just because you are not employed doesn't mean you can let yourself go. It will also leave a positive impression on the unemployment claims interviewer.
• Have a positive mental attitude when dealing with the interviewer.
—If treated rudely, do your best to rise above the situation, remembering the maxim about universal justice.
• Bring something to read/do while waiting.

If you are still reluctant about filing for unemployment insurance or want more information, we suggest reading the book, *"How to Collect Unemployment Benefits: Complete Information for All 50 States,"* by Raymond Avrutis (Prentice-Hall, 1983).

Now use the space below to write down the address and phone number of your local unemployment office and the name of your contact person.

Record of Tax-deductible Costs

Job hunting incurs expenses. Many of these can be deducted from your taxable income as a miscellaneous itemized deduction if the total amount of deductions exceeds two percent of the taxpayer's adjusted gross income, based on the Tax Reform Act of 1986 (Stephen J. Shay CPA, Shay & Associates, Laguna Hills, CA. 92653). Place all receipts in a manila envelope marked "Tax-Deductible Receipts." Write on your receipts the following information:

> Date
> Purpose
> Person contacted

You may find it useful to summarize all expenses weekly so all your records are neat and orderly for tax preparation time.

The worksheet on the following page will help you in this task. Additional copies of this form are available in Appendix C.

Job-search Expenses

Sample

On a weekly basis summarize all expenses on this form. At tax time your job will be much easier. A supply of this form is in Appendix C.

Date	Item	Cost	Method of Payment
8/5	Resume typeset & 100 copies	$48.62	Ck # 120
8/16	Lunch w. Sally Martin Imperial Bank	$18.31	American Express
8/17	Breakfast with Rich Wing	$12.17	American Express
8/20	Drove to USC Placement Office	120 miles @ 20¢/mi	
	Lunch with Jeff Atkins Placement Director	$13.18	American Express
8/25	ASTD Luncheon	$10.00	Check # 151
8/26	Drinks with Ingrid Moss, Westbrook Personnel	$10.14	Visa
8/27	PSA Roundtrip to Bay Area interview w BofA	$59—	American Express
8/28	Andrews Hotel Oakland, CA	$65.35	American Express

Going into Business for Yourself

We advise caution on starting your own business. The odds against successfully starting a business are high and require a tremendous amount of energy, capital, persistence, skill, and time. If you do wish to investigate going into business for yourself, we recommend contacting your local office of the Small Business Administration for a free checklist of qualities you will need to be successful. Universities in some areas are now putting on seminars on entrepreneurship.

PART 3

Finding That New Job

Your Present State of Mind

It's time to see how you are feeling again. Don't look at the results from the first time you did this exercise. Do this exercise as if this were the first time. Just react to the words listed below.

INSTRUCTIONS:

Check (√) which of the following emotions you presently feel:

___ Anger	___ Tearful	___ Grumpy
___ Bitter	___ What's next?	___ Heroic
___ Outrage	___ Finality	___ Hideous
___ Hurt	___ Tight chested	___ Horrible
___ Shock	___ Freedom	___ Ignorant
___ Disbelief	___ Fright	___ Imbecile
___ Anxiety	___ Autonomous	___ Inactive
___ Depressed	___ Argumentative	___ Incapacitated
___ Self-doubt	___ Apprehensive	___ Incisive
___ Humiliation	___ Ambiguous	___ Inspired
___ Shame	___ Abnormal	___ Jovial
___ Fear	___ Detached	___ Lavish
___ Relief	___ Docile	___ Lonesome
___ Conclusion	___ Dogmatic	___ Lovable
___ Beaten	___ Elation	___ Malicious
___ Loser	___ Endless	___ Moody
___ Whole	___ Feeble	___ Obsolete
___ Confusion	___ Forgiving	___ Paranoia

59

____ Chaotic	____ Free	____ Perplexed
____ Comatose	____ Frolic	____ Rejuvenated
____ Calm	____ Futile	____ Scapegoat
____ Cohesive	____ Strong	
____ Other _____		
(Specify)		

The first stage of grieving is shock/denial. Some words that describe this stage are:

> Confusion, Chaotic, Comatose, What's next?, Apprehensive, Ambiguous, Detached, Docile, Endless, Feeble, Perplexed, Ignorant, Imbecile, Inactive, Incapacitated, Obsolete, Scapegoat, Shock, and Disbelief.

The second stage of grieving is anger/depression. Some words that describe this stage are:

> Anxiety, Self-doubt, Fear, Tight-chested, Abnormal, Paranoia, Hurt, Depression, Beaten, Tearful, Lonesome, Anger, Bitterness, Outrage, Humiliation, Shame, Loser, Argumentative, Dogmatic, Futile, Grumpy, Hideous, Horrible, Malicious, Moody.

The third stage of grieving is understanding/acceptance. Some words that describe this stage are:

> Relief, Conclusion, Whole, Calm, Cohesive, Finality, Freedom, Autonomous, Elation, Forgiving, Free, Frolic, Heroic, Incisive, Inspired, Jovial, Lavish, Lovable, Rejuvenated, Strong.

Take a look at the items you checked ($\sqrt{}$). Do you see a pattern? Are the words you checked in one stage more than another? Or do you have equal amount of checks in all three stages?

Now go back and compare your answers to the first time you did this exercise. Has there been any improvement? Make a few notes about that improvement.

If not, go back and review your personal journals. Have you been taking good care of yourself? What special "treats" have you given yourself? Review what you have accomplished each day and take pride in your achievements. Review your Accomplishment/Achievements exercise and think about the positives in your life. If you find yourself still in stage one of the grieving process, shock/denial, we recommend that you spend time dealing with the reality that it happened to you. Find some outlets to release your anger, and go on with life. Let go of the anger; that anger will cripple your job-hunting efforts.

Remember, how you experience the grieving process is different for each person. The important issue is to know where you are within the process. After you have reached stage three, your outlook on life will become positive and allow you to project a positive self-image during your job search.

If you find that none of these words describe your current frame of mind, and are more positive, then good for you! You are on the right track. So let's get started on finding that new job.

Finding That New Job

In our society, our work—what we do for a living—defines who we are and what our status is. Work can be a means to an end, a paycheck, or it can mean much more, something that is an extension of ourselves. You are now faced with an opportunity to do something you always wanted to do. Our advice is to take advantage of that opportunity. If you really like what you're doing, your chances for being successful at it are phenomenally greater.

Changing jobs or careers is a big step. There's excitement at having a new beginning, but there is also a fair amount of doubt and uncertainty—change is not easy. However, the process of change can be made a lot more comfortable if you develop a Personal Marketing Plan. Realize that you and your skills are a product. You must focus on your best selling points and decide how you will market yourself. You have already completed the first step in developing your Personal Marketing Plan—to know the product, in section one, Taking Good Care of Yourself.

The second part of developing a Personal Marketing Plan is to decide what is the best work choice for you. The materials presented here are meant to be a starting point, helping to make the very important decisions about what course of action is best for you. In this section, you'll have the opportunity to:

- Create your Preferred-Job Profile;
- Create your Personal Action Plan
- Prepare for the interview process.

"*L*ife yields only to the conqueror.
Never accept what can be gained by giving in.
You will be living off stolen goods,
and your muscles will atrophy."
Dag Hammarskjold, *Markings*[5]

Your Personal Marketing Plan

There are basically two methods of job hunting. The first is the "traditional" method, the one you're probably most familiar with: you check want ads, employment agencies, recruiters, and send résumés. This method works well for some people, but before you begin your search with the traditional methods, look at some research from the Bureau of Labor Statistics. It becomes clear that the traditional methods—ads and agencies—are not the most effective way to find a job.

HOW AMERICANS LOOK FOR WORK

Applied Directly to Employer	66.0%
Asked Friends:	
About jobs where they work	50.8%
About jobs elsewhere	41.9%
Asked Relatives:	
About jobs where they work	28.4%
About jobs elsewhere	27.3%

Answered Newspaper Ads:

Local	45.9%
Nonlocal	11.7%
Private Employment Agency	21.0%
State Employment Service	33.5%
Civil Service Test	15.3%
School Placement Office	12.5%

HOW AMERICANS OBTAIN WORK

Applied Directly to Employer	34.9%
Asked Friends or Relatives:	
About jobs where they work	18.5%
About jobs elsewhere	7.7%
Answered Newspaper Ads	13.5%
Private Employment Agency	5.6%
State Employment Agency	5.1%
Other	11.7%
Total	100.0%

The second method of finding a job is one that involves "homework" and planning on your part. Primarily, it gives you the element of control in the job-search process, rather than relying on other sources to provide information about jobs. You become the one who makes direct contact with decision makers in companies you'd like to work for.

To better understand the "nontraditional" methods of finding a job, a distinction must be made between those jobs that are *vacant* and those that are potentially *open*. A "job vacancy" is a position that is empty. Vacancies are generally announced through formal channels such as newspaper ads and agencies. A "job opening," however, is a position that is still being worked, but will be open in the future. For example, an employer may want to promote someone, but hesitates because he wants a replacement to make a smooth transition. The vast majority of "job openings" are unannounced. On any given day, 85 percent of the job openings are not advertised in public formats such as newspapers. The best way of accessing them is through personal, direct contact with an employer or through people you know.

Therefore, the nontraditional job-search methods focus on two key elements:

> Expanding your search to "job openings"
> AND
> Establishing direct contact with decision makers.

There are four parts to the "nontraditional" job search method.

1. Decide whom you want to work for.
Have a thorough understanding of your skills and the type of job environment you would like to work in. For example, you can be a computer programmer in an engineering firm, or you might want to use that skill in a retail establishment.

We will step you through this process by completing the PREFERRED-JOB-PROFILE WORKSHEET.

2. Discover job openings using as many sources as possible.
In this case, the telephone will be your ally. You need to advertise the fact that you are looking for a job. Talk to your friends and people you know. A conversation with the mechanic who works on your car or even the checker at the grocery store can reveal job leads—but you've got to advertise and spread the word.

Other ways to discover Job Openings:
  • Attend local meeting of trade and professional organizations;

- Listen for news of local companies that are expanding or reorganizing, or of new companies coming to town;

- Read the newspaper and look for the following things:
    —Increased business demands
    —Plant relocations
    —Retirement announcements
    —New management
    —New inventions
    —New products
    —Terminations or layoffs
  It may be hard to believe, but every one of these things causes turmoil in the world of work, and that translates to needing new or different people to do the job.

- Use business directories to develop a list of companies to call. See the appendix for our suggestions.

3. Gather information about the company in preparation for the interview.
Just as you are flattered when someone takes the time to find out something about you, an employer's interest is peaked when you show that you've taken some time to find out about the company.

Business directories, trade journals, the financial section of the newspaper, annual reports, and former or current company employees can reveal useful information about a company. A list of some of the more useful directories is in the appendix.

Remember, every decision maker has opportunities which he or she is seeking to maximize. The key to getting the job will be to show the decision maker that you have just the right expertise that will help him or her make the operation run smoothly.

4. Get to the "Decision Maker!"

Decision makers are those people who have the power to hire you. Occasionally it might be the personnel department, but most often it is the person for whom you will actually work or the department head.

To get to the decision maker, you need to know how to get around the "receptionist." The role "receptionist" is defined as anyone who stands between you and the person doing the hiring. So it could be a secretary, another employee, the personnel department, or anyone you talk to on the phone who does not have the power to hire you. The section entitled "Telephone Techniques" will give you some other tips on how to use the phone in your job search.

So, what does all this mean? Should you use only nontraditional job-search methods? Or use both?

We recommend using both traditional and nontraditional job-search methods. You should monitor how much of your time is spent responding to newspaper ads versus direct contact. The payoff is in nontraditional job-search methods, particularly for professional and managerial jobs. Less than 10 percent of professional and managerial jobs are advertised.

Your Job Profile

Remember that you have a lot of control in the job-search process. Not only do you want someone to hire you, but you want to be hired for a job that will be satisfying and make you a happy, fulfilled individual. This exercise is designed to help you create a job profile for your ideal job. It should take into account your major strengths (skills you do well and enjoy) and also those conditions that will *add* to your personal and professional satisfaction.

To create your Job Profile:

1. List the jobs that you have held, or major areas of job responsibility that seemed to take the majority of your time (refer back to your SKILLS-ANALYSIS WORK-SHEETS).

2. For each job/area of responsibility, list the pros and cons. Try to have at least five for each area.

3. Then go back and circle the items that are most important to you.

A SAMPLE JOB-PROFILE CHART

	PROS	CONS
Job 1 Teacher	Working with people & children Short work year Helping people learn High self-confidence Good peer group	Understaffed Low pay Long hours Repetitive subjects
Job 2 Personnel Manager	Opportunity to interact with all parts of the organization Dealing with people Helping role	Staff position A lot of detail work May not be fully appreciated
Job 3		

Job-profile Worksheet

	PROS	CONS
JOB 1		
JOB 2		
JOB 3		
JOB 4		

JOB 5		
JOB 6		
JOB 7		

"Far better it is to dare mighty things, to win glorious triumphs, even though checkered by failure, than to rank with those poor spirits who neither enjoy much nor suffer much, because they live in the gray twilight that knows not victory nor defeat."
Theodore Roosevelt, *Familiar Quotations*[6]

Jobs and Bosses Worksheet

Your boss influences your growth and self-esteem, provides the tone and direction on a daily basis, and provides the tools to achieve both the goals of the organization and your own personal goals. Considering you could spend up to forty or fifty waking hours a week with this person let's define what a good boss is to you.

INSTRUCTIONS:

Look back at the jobs you have had in the past (JOB-PRO-FILE WORKSHEET) and describe:

Your best boss: _____

_____

_____

_____

_____

_____

_____

Your worst boss: _____

_____

_____

_____

_____

_____

_____

Here is a list of adjectives to consider while you describe the "good" boss as clearly as possible.

Tactful	Candid	Curious
Dependable	Conscientious	Insightful
Impulsive	Versatile	Empathetic
Adventuresome	Driving	Unique
High-energy	Risk-taking	Calm
Fair	Flexible	Patient
Tolerant	Creative	Neat
Attentive to details	Reliable	Firm
Diplomatic	Imaginative	Humorous
Competent	Expert	Punctual
Self-confident	Objective	Authentic
Honest	Astute	Poised
Sincere	Reliable	Outgoing
Loyal	Successful	

Now summarize, using short sentences or adjectives, what type of boss you want.

_____

_____

_____

_____

_____

_____

_____

_____

Now review your list of adjectives/short sentences and prioritize the attributes. This step is necessary so that you can make choices easily when trying to make a decision about accepting a position.

Now that you know what type of boss you want, the question becomes how you will recognize these qualities in an interview.

List each adjective you selected, and then write down how you can determine if someone has that quality. This may seem time-consuming now, but will save you a lot of effort when it comes down to interviewing.

_____

_____

_____

_____

_____

_____

_____

_____

Work-preferences Worksheet

Another consideration is the type of organization where you would like to work. To help you think about these different types, please complete the following exercise.

INSTRUCTIONS:

Place a check (√) by your preferred kinds of organizations.

___ Small	___ Publicly owned
___ Medium	___ Your Own Company
___ Large	___ Domestic
___ Centralized	___ International
___ Decentralized	___ Retail
___ Governmental	___ Wholesale
___ Private Sector	___ Service
___ Nonprofit	___ Manufacturing
___ Profit-making	___ Processing
___ Privately held	___ Distribution

Describe in one sentence the type of company you want to work for:

_____

_____

_____

_____

This information will help you narrow down your focus when using the business directories listed in the appendix.

Job-parameters Worksheet

In the early stages of your job search you are encouraged not to set limitations on potential jobs. Our reasoning is based upon the following:

- You can gain valuable experience from job interviews.
- You will gather information on the labor market.
- Each successive interview is a potential referral to other openings.

However, it is useful to answer the following items for later, when you are trying to narrow down your choices.

- Geographic preferences:

- Unacceptable locations:

- Amount of acceptable travel:

____ 0% ____ 25% ____ 50% ____ More than 50%

- Commuting distance you are willing to travel:

    ____ Miles ____ Time

- Minimum salary acceptable: $_____ hour
                               $_____ week
                               $_____ month
                               $_____ year

- Number of hours you are willing to work: _____ hours/week.

Job-titles and -images
Worksheet

List all the job titles that turn you on, interest you, made you envious, or that you admire. For each title list all the images that come to mind when you think about that job —both positive and negative.

Job Title: _____

Images: _____

_____

Job Title: _____

Images: _____

_____

Job Title: _____

Images: _____

_____

Job Title: _____

Images: _____

_____

Job Title: _____

Images: _____

_____

Circle the three images that are most important to you.

Career- and job-title Worksheet

The next step is to make a list of the specific careers that you believe offer you the greatest potential for fulfilling your needs. If you have a difficult time coming up with job titles don't worry—lots of people do.

INSTRUCTIONS:

Make up your own list of careers by reading the Sunday classified advertisements. Don't be judgmental, just write down all the different titles. If you want additional careers, refer to Appendix A for recommended career directories:

_____   _____   _____

_____   _____   _____

_____   _____   _____

_____   _____   _____

_____   _____   _____

_____   _____   _____

_____   _____   _____

_____   _____   _____

_____   _____   _____

_____   _____   _____

_____   _____   _____

_____   _____   _____

_____   _____   _____

_____   _____   _____
_____   _____   _____
_____   _____   _____
_____   _____   _____
_____   _____   _____
_____   _____   _____
_____   _____   _____
_____   _____   _____
_____   _____   _____
_____   _____   _____
_____   _____   _____
_____   _____   _____
_____   _____   _____

If you haven't been able to fill in all the spaces you either are:

- being too judgmental.
- living in a small town (use two papers or go to library for career directories).
- think this is stupid.

Remember you are your own limitation. If you don't let yourself see what is available and then look at the skill to get there, you will always be in a rut.

When you are satisfied with the number of career or job titles that you listed go back and place an asterisk (*) on the ones that are the most interesting to you.

Preferred-job-profile Worksheet

Let's summarize your ideal job profile from the information you have provided on the previous exercises by completing the following sentences:

1. Refer to JOB-PROFILE WORKSHEET:
   The best job for me would be one where I ...

2. Refer to JOBS-AND-BOSSES WORKSHEET:
   The type of boss I want is ...

3. Refer to WORK-PREFERENCES WORKSHEET:
   The types of organizations I want to work in are ...

4. Refer to JOB-PARAMETERS WORKSHEET:
   The job parameters that are most important to me are ...

5. Refer to JOB-TITLES AND -IMAGES WORKSHEET:
   The images I want to have in my new job are ...

6. Refer to CAREER- AND JOB-TITLE WORKSHEET:
   The job titles that excite me the most are ...

Job-search Action Plan

It is necessary to go about the job-search process systematically. A carefully thought-out Action Plan will help you avoid leaving any base uncovered. An Action Plan is a series of steps you take to reach your goal. Include in your action plan the following types of information:

- The date you will begin your job search, career change.
- The hours per day you will spend in the search (many professionals suggest an unemployed person spend eight hours per day—remember, it's your job right now).
- A date to have your updated résumé and list of references typed and ready.
- A list of trade or professional courses you may need including where, when, and availability.
- A list of companies you would like to work for (don't hesitate to list them all).
- A list of people who can help you either get a job or who can refer you to someone who can.
- A list of the resources you will use to aid you in your search (these can be friends, professionals, books, worksheets).
- Determine an approximate date when each item will be completed.

Most importantly, make the action plan a workable one for you. Each step of the plan should move you closer to your work goal. Have it reviewed by someone who can offer suggestions on how to improve it.

The JOB-SEARCH ACTION-PLAN WORKSHEET is a handy form that organizes all your steps in one place and becomes an easy reference document for what you have accomplished. A sample Action Plan is on the next page.

Job-search Action-plan Worksheet

Sample

DATE	ACTION
8/4	Review old resume. Complete "Gathering Facts section of workbook.
8/7	Complete Networking Worksheet. List all professional contacts who can help.
8/10	Determine long-term goals — what type of job do I want? Complete Section I of book by end of week.
8/12	Tell my family that I am being laid off.
8/14	Prepare a tight budget scaling back to bare essentials. Use financial Worksheet pg. 68
8/15	Register with professional agency
8/16	Start calling friends for referrals & info. Call 5 people a day.
8/17	Check classifieds in professional journals & major newspapers. Allow 2 hrs in library.
8/18	Have first draft of Resume done
8/20	Call & meet with University alumni placement office
8/24	Figure out how to find business directories at library
8/25	Attend professional training society luncheon. Get mailing list

In addition to your Action Plan we have found the following job-search strategy useful:

1. Respond to ads.
   - Read the New York Times, Wall Street Journal, local papers, professional trade magazines for jobs you have targeted.
   - Use Classified-Ad Worksheet (page 84).
   - Avoid Personnel Departments if possible.
   - Tailor cover letter and résumé, and address them directly to person doing the hiring.
2. Send letters to search firms and employment agencies.
   - Go to private employment agencies.
   - Go to federal/state job services.
   - Use Agency-Contact Worksheet (page 86).
3. Direct-company contact.
   - Identify organizations that have positions/careers that you have targeted.
   - Tailor letters.
   - Use Direct-Company-Contact Worksheet (page 85).
4. Networking.
   - Ask friends, relatives, teachers, and other professional referrals about jobs where they work.
   - Tailor referral letters and thank-you letters.
   - Use Networking Worksheet (page 126).

"Really marvelous experiences occur infrequently,
are of brief duration,
and are rarely on schedule."
Sol Gordon, *The New You: A Book Of Life*[7]

---

5. Other.
   - Contact college placement offices.
   - Go to union hiring halls.
   - Work through a job-search program.
   - Go to Forty Plus (job search program for 40 and over).

Most people only answer a couple of ads and maybe send a few résumés, and then wait and get depressed. The non-traditional job search incorporates all of the methods listed above. The more you do the better off you will be.

To Get Started You Will Need:

   - A good appointment calendar
   - Maps of potential areas of employment
   - Telephone-answering service or answering machine
   - Tape
   - Scissors
   - Business stationery
   - Personal stationery
   - Current résumé
   - Job-Search Action-Plan Worksheet
   - Networking Worksheet
   - Classified-Ad Worksheet
   - Direct-Company-Contact Worksheet
   - Agency-Contact Worksheet

An example of the last three worksheets and how they are used is provided for you on the following pages. Additional copies of each worksheet are in Appendix C.

Classified-ad Worksheet

Cut out and tape here each classified advertisement to which you respond. Be sure to read the ad carefully, noting the specifications for the job and key information about applying. Your cover letter should address how you meet the requirements and what value you can bring to the organization.

Where ad listed & date: _Wall Street Journal 9/8_
Response:

    Résumé Sent: (date) _9/8_

    Confirmation Résumé Received: (date)

    Reject Letter Received: (date)

    Screening Phone Call: (date)

    Interview Scheduled: (date)

    Follow-Up Letter Sent: (date)

    Follow-Up Phone Call: (date)

    Offer Made: (date)

Comments: _____

_____

_____

_____

Direct-company-contact Worksheet

Sample

List a Minimum of 100 Firms to Contact

Name, Address, and Phone Number of Company	Name of Person to Contact and Title	Date Contacted	Response
ARA 271 ConsTuTion Ave Philadelphia , PA 17518	Bill Bell President **Comments:** Resume & letter mailed 8/20 follow up on 8/30		
Mazda Motors 512 S. Main St. Cerritos, CA 92307 213/ 555-1212	Yoshio Obaiashi, V.P. Administration **Comments:** Resume & letter mailed 8/31 Follow-up phone 9/7 Interview scheduled 9/8	8/31	INTERESTED
Dyna Drill 13001 Maybelle St Houston, Texas 817/555-1333	Hustin Smith H.R. Director **Comments:** Resume & letter mailed 9/16 Relocation ? potential referral to another division.	9/15 -phone	Has position
Western Airlines 582 Ocean Ave. San Jose, CA 92642 312/551-2121	**Comments:** Resume & letter mailed 8/12		no response

85

Agency-contact Worksheet

Use a separate worksheet for each agency contacted, and list employers they send you to.

Westbrook Personnel Agency, 714 Balboa, SD. CA 92109, 255-1939 Ingrid Moss

Agency Name, Address, Telephone Number, and contact person.

	Date Resume Mailed	Type of Response	Recommended Follow-up, i.e., Telephone Call, Visit, Etc.	Referrals
Company: *Studio One*	*9/20*	*Resume*	*Call 9/7*	
Address: *P.O. Box 130*				
San Francisco, CA 92123				
	Comments:			
Telephone:				
415/661-1212				
Company: _____	_____	_____	_____	_____
Address: _____				
_____				
Telephone: _____	**Comments:**			
_____				
Company: _____	_____	_____	_____	_____
Address: _____				
_____				
Telephone: _____	**Comments:**			
_____				

Telephone Techniques

Most job hunters turn shy when faced with using the phone to call strangers. Even the most outgoing, friendly person feels uneasy and often intimidated by the task. Mastery of the telephone is essential to the success of your job search. Establishing contacts with potential employers, peers, and friends is how you get information about the unadvertised job market. Using the telephone you could easily reach twenty people a day. How many people can you reach by just dropping in? How many résumés can you afford to mail out? As you can see, the phone needs to become your best friend.

GENERAL TIPS:

- Schedule your calls to begin at a certain time each day. It's much harder to procrastinate if you have established a pattern.
- We recommend calling Tuesday through Friday mornings. Mondays are unpredictable and should be avoided. Often Mondays are spent processing new hires, attending staff meetings, and dealing with problems from the weekend, while the executive was away. Friday afternoons are even worse, that's when "exit interviews" are most often occurring.
- Set a daily and weekly goal. Once you have gotten over your fear of the phone, twenty or thirty calls a day is reasonable.
- Take a break after three or five calls and reward yourself. This is a difficult task, so be good to yourself.
- Do not admit you are looking for a job unless you are responding to an ad.
- Your goal in calling is to talk to a particular person about a certain topic, not to ask for a job.

- Call just before or right after normal business hours. Many times the secretary/receptionist has gone home and the "boss" answers the phone.
- Don't leave your name and number if you couldn't get through to the decision maker. This prevents you from making more calls, keeping your line open. You should call back at a more convenient time, when you are prepared to initiate the call.
- Preparation is everything.

Try, try, try, again. Remember this is how you will discover those other 85 percent of unadvertised jobs.

HOW TO USE THE PHONE TO GET AN INTERVIEW:

1. Research twenty-five names and phone numbers of firms that could hire or have hired someone in the position you are interested in.

2. Find out who the decision maker is. The person who has the authority to hire.

3. Call the decision maker until you get through.

4. Communicate a clear value and ask for a meeting.

5. If the answer is yes, prepare yourself for the meeting by preparing the questions you want to ask.

6. If the answer is no, ask if you can send a résumé. If he/she is not interested, scratch it off as one more no and try someone else. If they do want a résumé send it with a well thought-out, personalized cover letter.

7. A week after you have sent your résumé, call again to make sure he/she has received it. Ask again for a meeting.

Remember, this is the most effective way to reach a large number of people, and job hunting is a numbers game.

EXAMPLE OF TRYING-TO-OBTAIN-AN-INTERVIEW PHONE CALL:

Call One:
The first call would be placed to the main telephone number of a company. You want to obtain the name of the person who is in charge of the department you are interested in. The correct spelling of that name. The person's exact title. The direct phone number or extension number.

Call Two
Receptionist: Mr. Wright's office.
You: I'd like to speak with Mr. Wright.
Receptionist: May I ask what this is regarding?
You: I was referred by Mr. Hall (use referral if you have one)
   OR:
I would like some information about the pro forma system.
   OR:
This is a personal call.
(THE ASSUMPTION HERE IS YOU HAVE PRE-PLANNED THIS CALL AND TARGETED THIS EMPLOYER. THIS MEANS YOU ALREADY KNOW THAT THIS EMPLOYER HAS JUST OR WILL AUTOMATE THE FINANCIAL FUNCTION WITH THE PRO FORMA SYSTEM. YOUR KEY TO GETTING AN INTERVIEW IS MAKING YOURSELF VALUABLE—YOUR EXPERTISE—TO THE POTENTIAL EMPLOYER.)
Receptionist: Just a moment.

Once you have established contact, verify that he/she is the right person to talk to and that he/she has a few moments to talk. Then within the first minute of the conversation communicate something about yourself which is an irresistible value to the employer.

You: Mr. Wright, my name is Fred Moss, do you have a few moments?
If no:
   When would be a good time to call back to talk about how you automated the financial system?

If yes:

I understand that you have just automated your monthly reports using the pro forma system?

Mr. Wright: Yes, we have.

You: You'll like the new system. I have worked with the pro forma system for five years. Once your people have gotten used to the new way, their jobs will be much easier.

Mr. Wright: I hope so. Right now things are pretty unsettled.

You: I'm sure it is. I presented an orientation for both the financial people and the managers who had to use the new reports. It really helped them to understand what additional information and opportunities they had with the new system.

Mr. Wright: Who did you say you were?

You: I am Fred Moss. I can help you with some of the transition issues using the pro forma system. I would be glad to meet with you to discuss this further.

If the employer begins interviewing you on the phone, answer his/her questions politely and briefly, then ask to meet in person to explain your qualifications more fully. Always answer the questions, but finish by asking for a meeting.

HOW TO USE THE PHONE TO GET INFORMATION INTERVIEW:

1. Research twenty-five names and phone numbers of firms that have people who have the same type of skills you do.

2. You do not want to talk to the decision maker, but the person who has information about using certain skills or knowledge you want.

3. Communicate clearly what it is you want to know and ask for a meeting. Always have your questions prepared in advance.

4. Never ask for a job during an information-gathering phone call or meeting.

5. Keep track of who you called, when and about what (see NETWORKING WORKSHEET).

6. Types of questions to ask:
   - Recommendations or referrals to employers.
   - To review or critique your résumé.
   - An introduction to decision makers in firms related to your needs.
   - Information interview with executives in your field of interest.
   - Suggestions about career choices for you.
   - Referral to specific information sources.
   - Knowledge about pending management changes in companies.
   - Information about openings that are about to be advertised.
   - Names of companies that have developed new products or have certain problems they are trying to solve.
   - Suggestions on how to help you with certain problems.

7. Follow up with a phone call to keep your source informed on your progress and or to thank him for help.

EXAMPLE OF INFORMATION CALL:

> *Voice:* Good afternoon, Bonanza International. May I help you?
> *You:* This is John Romero and I need to speak with the Director of Training, but I have misplaced his name. Could you help me?
> *Voice:* Yes, that would be Ted Brollini.
> *You:* Oh, yes and thank you. Could you please transfer this call? Oh, and does he have a direct line, in case we're disconnected?
> *Voice:* Yes, that's extension 212. I'll transfer you now.
> *Secretary:* Mr. Brollini's office.
> *You:* Yes, this is Jim. Could you put me through to Ted please? I need to talk to him right away.

Secretary: Just a moment, please.

Voice: This is Ted Brollini.

You: Hello, This is John Romero. You and I have never met and I'm calling because of some information I am trying to gather. Do you have a few minutes or should I call later?

Voice: Go ahead.

You: I am currently an HRD Consultant in the personnel area and am planning a career change in the near future. I need help defining alternatives in the training and development field. Since you are well respected in the industry I felt you would be able to provide me with that information. Besides, I've heard so much about your organization. Would it be possible to see you tomorrow morning or I have some time available at the end of the week if that would be better?

Voice: Well, Ted. Tuesday is actually better for me.

Your Résumé

Now that you have spent time identifying your personal strengths, analyzing your work experiences, and creating a personal marketing plan, you are ready for the next step, the résumé.

WHAT IS A RÉSUMÉ?

A résumé is a catalog of your qualifications. Its purpose is to convince a prospective employer that you should be invited for a job interview. You have something to sell—your skills. Hence, a résumé is a personal advertisement that outlines your qualifications for a particular job. Because you are a unique person, your résumé will be a distinct presentation of your skills and abilities, experience, and personality. The information you choose to include and the arrangement of the material on the page are critical in providing the first impression of you to an employer. In addition, the résumé shows the employer how you do things, especially written communication, which is so important in today's world. But that's not all. A résumé can also demonstrate your own self-worth and how thoroughly you get the job done. To impress a busy employer, a résumé should be neat, brief, and accomplishment/results oriented. Remember, you never get a second chance to make a good first impression.

WHO SHOULD HAVE A RÉSUMÉ?

Today, with increased specialization and mobility, the use of résumés extends to all levels and types of jobs. Regardless of your type or scope of your job, you probably need a résumé unless this happens: you show up to interview, get hired, and start work the same day.

ARE THERE GUIDELINES IN PREPARING A RÉSUMÉ?

There are no absolutes in the preparation of a résumé. However, there are certain factors that contribute significantly to its effectiveness. The résumés that most often produce exceptional results are those that are clean and distinctive in appearance. Your résumé should be an attention-getter, which is prepared in a concise and professional manner. THE PURPOSE OF A RÉSUMÉ IS TO PEAK THE EMPLOYER'S INTEREST IN SEEING YOU, NOT TO PROVIDE EVERY DETAIL OF YOUR SKILLS AND BACKGROUND. Most experts agree upon the following guidelines for résumé preparation:

Length:
A one-page résumé is best. A résumé is not an autobiography but a capsule of significant points about your background.

Spatial Arrangement:

Research shows that personnel specialists spend an average of twelve seconds on each résumé. Make your résumé clear and easily read. Avoid crowding information on a page. Experiment with different arrangements of headlines and test to find one you like. Some guidelines are:

- Use the best typewriter you can get your hands on. If you have a PC (personal computer) at home make sure your printer is letter quality. Do NOT use a dot matrix printer. It's not a professional image.
- Use a new, dark typewriter ribbon so you can get the cleanest, clearest image possible.
- Use at least one-inch margins on all sides.
- Use single space for text and double space between paragraphs.
- Use uppercase letters for headings or titles that are important.
- Use indentation to separate different types of information. This makes the reader's job easier.
- Use "bullets" (• or . or *) to highlight key results or accomplishments. Boldfaced type can also be used to highlight.
- Use lots of "white space" or "air." This means that you should see more white paper (empty space) than print. White space is a way of accenting what is important, and, best yet, it is restful on the reader's eye and mind.

Professional Appearance:

There is no excuse for a single error on a résumé. Accurate spelling, consistent punctuation, and neat typing are extremely important. Some guidelines are:

- Have several people edit and critique for grammar, spelling, and punctuation. You'll be surprised how

many errors skipped by you. It really is a difficult job to edit your own work.
- Have the résumé reproduced professionally. We recommend a photo-offset process. This will maintain the clarity and crispness of the original. DO NOT duplicate on a home or office photocopier.
- Use a high-quality paper stock. You can use white, ivory, buff, or off-white.
- Print at least a hundred copies. Don't waste your time going back and forth to the printer.
- Purchase an extra ream of paper (500 sheets) that matches the paper stock of the résumé. You will use this paper for cover letters.

Order of Presentation:
There is no single prescribed format for a résumé. The most essential elements are your name, address, and telephone number prominently displayed at the top of the page. Other sections of information vary according to individual tastes and backgrounds. They usually include the following topics:

Career Goal/Objective:
You must be as specific as possible in identifying the type of position you are seeking. Avoid generalities such as,

"I want to work with people"
"Seeking a challenging position that will utilize my background and education."

If you are applying for a variety of jobs, you have several options.

—You may wish to prepare several résumés, each with a different objective.
—Indicate a general objective such as "Management Position" with more specific interests explained in individual cover letters.

—Omit an objective from the résumé altogether and state it only in the cover letter.

Education:
A brief outline of your education should include all colleges attended, in reverse chronological order, with dates, degrees granted, and major and minor areas of study. If your education or degree is within the last five years and industry-specific then it should appear in the upper half of the résumé. Otherwise place at the bottom half of the résumé.

Employment Experience:
Employers are favorably impressed by any work experience, regardless of its nature. Summer, part-time, and volunteer experience that supports your career objective should always be included. Indicate job title, name of organization, dates (month and year) and accomplishments. You should give most emphasis to jobs related to the type of position you are seeking at present; you may group together work experiences that are unrelated.

Use action verbs in phrases to describe your past accomplishments and results, such as:

- —planned meetings.
- —created outreach program.
- —organized records.
- —designed publicity announcements.

Remember, don't list duties. Duties are no more than obligations—they are not results.

Activities:
List all memberships and offices held in community organizations. Employers are looking for demonstrated leadership and a variety of interests.

Honors:
Note all honors, special awards, scholarships, and Dean's List recognitions accomplished while in school or on a job.

Personal Information:
Do not include any information that may screen you out such as:

—age.
—health.
—personal statistics (height, weight, sex).
—marital status.
—hobbies.

References:
Indicate that references will be furnished upon request. Do not list names and addresses on the résumé. References are generally not provided until requested by an employer. Besides, references are too precious to annoy, and you want to be able to contact them first. If you don't have any reference letters, begin developing a list of two or three professional associates who you feel confident will present your qualifications and abilities in a positive and beneficial way. Be sure these individuals are aware of their involvement in your employment search and agree to provide a reference for you.

Gathering the Facts to Prepare Your Résumé

At this point you are probably thinking, "Now what?" I have already detailed my skills (you have, haven't you?) what more do you want? The good news is this exercise is fun.

It's like Job Hunters Trivial Pursuit. This is where you list all the information concerning where you have worked, school hobbies, and so on. There will be far more information than you'll need for the actual résumé. This information, however, will be useful for completing employment applications.

<u>*INSTRUCTIONS:*</u>

Fill in the blanks. Have some fun with this—sort of stroll down memory lane.

Education & Training

High School:

Name of school(s): _____

Dates attended: _____

Date graduated or equivalence test: _____

Honors, awards, or special recognition: _____

Best subjects: _____

Extracurricular activities: _____

_____

_____

College (undergraduate):

Name of school: _____

Dates attended: _____

Date graduated: _____ Degree: _____

Major: _____ Minor: _____

Honors or awards: _____

Extracurricular activities: _____

_____

_____

College (graduate):

Name of school: _____

Dates attended: _____

Date graduated: _____   Degree: _____

Major: _____   Minor: _____

Honors or awards: _____

Extracurricular activities: _____

_____

_____

College (postgraduate):

Name of school: _____

Dates attended: _____

Date graduated: _____   Degree: _____

Major: _____   Minor: _____

Honors or awards: _____

Extracurricular activities: _____

_____

_____

Other Training:
List any vocational courses, internships, on-job training, workshops, seminars, or other formal training.

Course: _____   Date taken: _____

Skills learned: _____

Course: _____   Date taken: _____

Skills learned: _____

Course: _____ Date taken: _____
Skills learned: _____

Course: _____ Date taken: _____
Skills learned: _____

Course: _____ Date taken: _____
Skills learned: _____

Course: _____ Date taken: _____
Skills learned: _____

Hobbies

Hobby: _____ Accomplishment: _____
Hobby: _____ Accomplishment: _____
Hobby: _____ Accomplishment: _____
Hobby: _____ Accomplishment: _____

Part-Time Jobs

Employer: _____ Dates: _____
Job Title: _____ Supervisor's name: _____
Accomplishments: _____
Skills: _____

Employer: _____ Dates: _____
Job Title: _____ Supervisor's name: _____
Accomplishments: _____
Skills: _____

Employer: _____ Dates: _____
Job Title: _____ Supervisor's name: _____

Accomplishments: _____

Skills: _____

Employer: _____ Dates: _____

Job Title: _____ Supervisor's name: _____

Accomplishments: _____

Skills: _____

Full-Time Jobs

Employer: _____ Dates: _____

Job Title: _____ Supervisor's name: _____

Accomplishments: _____

Skills: _____

Employer: _____ Dates: _____

Job Title: _____ Supervisor's name: _____

Accomplishments: _____

Skills: _____

Employer: _____ Dates: _____

Job Title: _____ Supervisor's name: _____

Accomplishments: _____

Skills: _____

Employer: _____ Dates: _____

Job Title: _____ Supervisor's name: _____

Accomplishments: _____

Skills: _____

Employer: _____ Dates: _____

Job Title: _____ Supervisor's name: _____

Accomplishments: _____

Skills: _____

Honors, awards, special recognitions, and professional memberships:

_____

_____

_____

_____

References

Name: _____ Phone Number: _____

Title: _____ work _____

Address: _____

Name: _____ Phone Number: _____

Title: _____ work _____

Address: _____

Name: _____ Phone Number: _____

Title: _____ work _____

Address: _____

Name: _____ Phone Number: _____

Title: _____ work _____

Address: _____

Name: _____ Phone Number: _____

Title: _____ work _____

Address: _____

Types of Résumés

The two most common types of résumé use either the chronological or the functional format.

Chronological:
List all jobs in reverse order, with the most recent first. Titles and company names are emphasized. This format is very popular and the easiest to prepare. Use this type of format when:

- each position has been of progressively greater responsibility.
- if next step in your career is apparent.
- name of last employer adds prestige.
- if you are staying in the same field or industry.
- prior job titles are impressive.
- seeking employment in a traditional field (finance, education).

Functional:
This format lists work experiences in terms of one or more specific "functions" you wish to emphasize, such as Finance, Administration, or Support Services and gives the important contributions made in each function. Job dates, names of departments, and titles can be omitted or placed in a very brief list later in the résumé. This approach should support and tie closely to your stated career objectives. Use this type of format when:

- you are planning a career change.
- your carrer has been in reverse gear and you want to disguise that backward trend.
- most of your work has been consulting or temporary.
- you have had multiple different jobs.
- you want to disguise your age or an employment gap.

- you want to emphasize newly acquired skills.
- you are entering the job market for the first time.
- you are reentering the job market after a long absence.

If you feel that the chronological and functional formats are not for you, we recommend reading the book, *The Perfect Résumé,* by Tom Jackson. It is a very good step-by-step approach to résumé writing. He includes three other formats, the targeted format, a résumé alternative, and other creative alternatives.

Sample Résumés in Chronological Format

The following resumes are in a chronological format. Use this type of format when your career direction is clear and the job you have targeted matches your work history. The chronological format emphasizes employment continuity and career growth. It is particularly useful if the names of your previous employers are prestigious.

There are many layouts that can be used in the chronological format. However, notice that the job history is spelled out from the most recent job first, then it works backwards. Titles and organizations are emphasized with duties and accomplishments described.

Madeline Moore
2288 Cove Avenue
Fresno, CA 90027
714/777-1939

EDUCATION: MBA, Babson College
                   BA, Northeastern University, Accounting
                   AS, Northeastern University, Computer Sciences

EXPERIENCE:
1980–Present   **STANDARD VALVE CORPORATION.**   Fresno, California

                   ASSISTANT CONTROLLER — Supervises 17 professional accounting
                   and data processing personnel. Responsibility encompassing financial
                   planning, reporting and control — including general accounting; cost
                   accounting; financial analysis; the development of the annual budget
                   and budget controls, inventory reporting and analysis; internal audit;
                   plus all EDP operations.

                   ACCOMPLISHMENTS: Designed and installed a corporate–wide
                   plant computerized standard cost system. Implemented a program
                   for short-term investment of surplus funds. Decreased average age
                   of accounts receivable from 45 to 33 days.

1976–1980   **AMERICAN MACHINE-TOOL CORPORATION.**   Dayton, Ohio

                   PLANT CONTROLLER — Supervised 3 accountants. Prepared
                   manufacturing budgets, the financial and capital forecasts, standard
                   cost reports and monthly closings.

                   ACCOMPLISHMENTS: Successfully directed the standardization and
                   automation of the financial reporting and standard cost systems.

1970–1976   **UNITED PROCESS MACHINERY.**   Bow, New Hampshire

                   MANAGER OF ACCOUNTING (1974-1976)

                   ACCOMPLISHMENTS: Redesigned and partially automated A/P and
                   A/R systems resulting in the elimination of two clerical positions.

                   FINANCIAL ANALYST (1971-1974)

                   COST ANALYST (1970-1971)

ACTIVITIES: National Association of Accountants,
                   President New Hampshire Chapter

REFERENCES: Furnished upon request.

JACK MILLER
980 Klish Street
Chicago, Illinois   33152
(415) 577-2501

CAREER OBJECTIVE

Entry management position in the field of computer science with special emphasis in finance, marketing and/or forecasting.

EXPERIENCE

3/85–6/88

SENIOR SYSTEMS ANALYST/PROGRAMMER
Fotomat Corporation.   La Jolla, California
Analyze and correct software problems, support system. Debug system, update subroutines, modify programs, modify FMS form libraries. Write and tailor programs for accounting   personnel. Evaluate system's daily performance, control terminal usage, affront terminal users' problems, restore users' confidence.

8/81–3/85

SYSTEMS ANALYST/PROGRAMMER
General Atomic.   San Diego, California
Restructured accounting system to an Interactive Associates Internal FAS. Designed, enhanced, maintained batch and on-line Cobol applications. Constructed attribute dictionary, supervised financial analysis of accounts, set case controls. Designed screen layouts, defined video attributes, field descriptions, data names. Research, organized, wrote and published software user's Manuals. Authored and documented accounting procedures, administered terminal operation training.

2/81–6/81

SYSTEMS ANALYST ASSISTANCE, OPERATIONS RESEARCH
Honda Corporate Headquarters.   Gardena, California.
Conducted statistic and performance measurement test of the CICS system and its application to productivity and demand. Designed parts systems specifications for management approval. Analyzed current systems performance for deficiencies, reported corrective action requirements. Expanded system development background.

11/78–3/79

LABORATORY ASSISTANT
University of California.   Santa Barbara, California
Converted sample test data into assembler language. Abstracted research material for data files. Composed, reported and organized manuscripts for Political Science Department. Used IBM 360/370.

EDUCATION   B.A. University of California, Santa Barbara, June 1980
Computer Science and Business Economics

Suzanne P. Knight
153 Streamwood Drive
San Diego, CA   95062

Home (619) 555-1212   Work (619) 121-1212

PROFESSIONAL WORK EXPERIENCE

Butler Restaurants   August, 1982 to Present.
District Trainer.   Line position reporting to Area Operations Coordinator with
dotted line responsibilities to the Director of Training.   Conduct Manager Training
for forty-eight fast food restaurants through out Orange, Imperial and San Diego
counties.   Design and conduct train-the trainer sessions for the roll out of new
products and procedures.   Assist corporate on a variety of specific training projects
including   need   analysis,   employee   sensing,   and   the   design   of   an   performance
evaluation training program.

EDUCATION

1986   Certificate awarded, Laboratory Education Intern Program, University
        Associates, San Diego.
1982   Research Project, Carnegie Foundation, New York.
1982   M.A. Psychology, University of California, Berkeley.
1979   B.A. Finance, University of Southern California, Los Angeles.

MEMBERSHIPS

American Society for Training & Development,
OD Network.

REFERENCES AVAILABLE UPON REQUEST

JOE GREEN
1939 Via Aprilla
St. Louis, Missouri   30326
(916) 982-2387

**POSITION
SOUGHT**

A management position with responsibility for project design, control, and implementation, in producing effective management information system software packages.

EDUCATION:

BS Northwestern University
BA National University, Information Systems
MS Candidate, National University, Education

REVIEW OF WORK EXPERIENCES

**PROJECT
DESIGN:**

As a member of a design team, determined structure of an on-line system for insurance claims processing. Designed prototype installation to replace second-generation equipment, resulting in a three-fold increase in through-time efficiency and training lead-time.

**SYSTEMS
ANALYST:**

As a team member, wrote a proposal document for a 400 million dollar project involving large-scale conversion to an IBM hardware and operating systems. Responsible for detailed analysis of training needs, skills assessments, course designs, and logistic consideration. Designed and implemented claims processing system to define file structure and interaction, access paths, inquiry and file updating, both in interactive and batch modes. Defined and implemented application programs used for text editing, file creation, visual representation, graphics, perspective, and data transformation.

PROGRAMMER: Wrote application programs using wide scope of high-level compiler languages including COBOL, FORTRAN, ALGOL, BASIC, AND PL-1. Programs executed complex functions of motion simulation, perspective, data element capture, error detection, editing, and data retrieval.

**SPECIAL
QUALITIES:**

Skilled at designing user-oriented interactive systems. Considered an excellent communicator.

EMPLOYMENT: TRAINING ANALYST, Northrop Services, Inc.

PROGRAMMER ANALYST, Xycor, Inc.

DATA PROCESSING TECHNICIAN/SYSTEMS ANALYST, U. S. Navy

Sample Résumés in Functional Format

The following resumes are in a functional format. Use this type of format when your career direction is changing, or if you are entering the job market after a long period of time. The functional format allows you to emphasize strengths or abilities which may not be reflected by your work history. It is particularly useful if you want to hide repetition of job duties or a weak work history.

There are many layouts that can be used in the functional format. However, notice that the major areas of accomplishments and strength are highlighted and there should be a direct tie-in with your work objectives or targeted job. Previous employer names, job titles and employment dates can be left off.

SABRINA MONTALVO
1936 NARDO STREET
NEW YORK, NY 92075
(209) 755-1212

EXPERTISE
Office Management

CAPABILITIES
Able to accomplish tasks without supervision, flexible, works well under pressure.

QUALIFICATIONS
Managed an office and coordinated all funds for employer and employees; coordinated administrative matters with internal personnel; initiated and set up an efficient and organized filing/record system; scheduled appointments and received visitors, exercised judgment and social skills; drafted and composed necessary correspondence; supervised other clerical personnel.

Performed office bookkeeping, including payroll, accounts receivable and payable, tax deposits, and W-2 forms; reconciled company's bankbook balance; experienced in traffic and warehouse shipping procedures; typed financial statements, invoices, bills, and bills of lading (foreign and domestic); accurately prepared expense reports.

Prepared technical reports, including charts, graphs, and calculations; updated administrative and marketing manuals; typed and maintained technical reports, blueprints, and government specs; responsible for design, layout, and paste-up of activity and program flyers; make travel/conference arrangements and accommodations; obtained bids from office supply vendors for price comparison and submitted recommendations for contract award.

EMPLOYMENT EXPERIENCE

Muliti Image	May 1983 - May 1988
Specter Incorporated	Nov. 1979 - April 1982
Y.M.C.A.	Nov. 1978 - Nov. 1979

TECHNICAL SKILLS
Typing 70-80 wpm, Shorthand 110 wpm, Dictaphone, IBM 029 Keypunch, 10-key by touch, Telex, Bestetner Mimeograph, Addressograph.

SALLY MORIYAMA

1960 West Brown St.   o Houston, Texas   93710   o (616) 580-3322

Position Objective:

To obtain a position within a corporate environment, utilizing my experience as a corporate travel planner.

Qualifications:

- o Coordinate and organized the needs of groups ranging in size from 10 to 600.
- o Analyzed and effectively defined problems.
- o Provided training to new staff and explained programs and policies pertaining to the product.
- o Interfaced with accounting, finance and marketing departments.
- o Acted as trouble shooter between corporate staff and field departments; served as a liaison between management and other staff personnel.
- o Able to meet deadlines and work extremely well under pressure.
- o Excellent oral and written communication skills.
- o 12 years extensive public contact experience.
- o Utilized communication skills with agents from all over United States.
- o Willing to accept responsibility and learn quickly.

Education:

Loyola University, B.A., Sociology, minor Spanish; GPA 3.4, June 1972
Marymount Palos Verdes, A.A., Liberal Arts, June 1970
Xerox Professional Selling Skills Course, June 1982

Personal Data:

Avid reader; good knowledge of political and world events; sports enthusiast, and world traveler.

References & Job History:

Available upon request.

Mike J. White
6262 Hurd Court
San Diego, CA 92123
(619) 528-1212

OBJECTIVE: A position where both my scientific and managerial experience can contribute to a fast growing company.

EDUCATION:

BS Civil Engineering, University of Santa Clara, 1971
MS Oceanography, Scripps Inst. of Oceanography, 1978
PhD Marine Biology, Scripps Inst. of Oceanography, 1984

WORK EXPERIENCE:

Project Management:
Managed eight scientific projects. Authored twenty-five publications on topics ranging from remote sensing tools to reproductive strategies of fish and dolphin behavior. Coordinated project analysis for technology information systems for administrative offices scattered throughout the United States and Pacific Islands.

Leadership:
Served as ship's officer on three NOAA research vessels. Served as chief scientist of six survey units. Most recently field assignment was Commanding Officer of a 2000-ton, 215-foot fisheries research trawler operating in artic waters. Provide daily direction to three scientists and a staff of six non salaried workers.

Staff Advisor:
Prepared research plans, staffing and budget options for a wide variety of operations. Most recently developed long-range strategy for the incorporation of information technology into NOAA's research laboratories.

PROFESSIONAL LICENSES:

Professional Engineer, State of California
Land Surveyor, State of California
Master, United States Coast Guard

PUBLICATIONS & REFERENCES: Available on request.

Résumé Checklist

After you have written several drafts and before you duplicate your résumé, refer to this checklist as a final check.

_____ Total length one page.

_____ No spelling, grammar, or punctuation errors.

_____ Typing is neat and dark, no errors.

_____ Good use of "white space."

_____ Capitalization, bolding, underlining, and use of "bullets" are consistent.

_____ Name, address, and telephone number at top of résumé.

_____ Paragraphs no longer than eight to ten lines.

_____ All margins at least one inch.

_____ All statements are concise and direct.

_____ Results and accomplishments use action verbs.

_____ At least three people have critiqued and edited your résumé.

_____ No personal information (height, weight, age, sex).

_____ No salary information.

_____ No geographical preference unless it is a requirement.

_____ No references in résumé.

_____ Remove negative or explanatory remarks such as recently divorced, long illness, handicap.

Remember, the purpose of your résumé is to have an employer want to interview you. The way you do that is have your résumé state results and accomplishments that are of value to the company. The employer wants to know what value you can produce for them.

What Happens to Your Résumé?

Classified advertisements in major newspapers generate hundreds of responses. The first task of the recruiter is to reduce the number of résumés to a workable number. This can be done by separating the résumés into the following three categories:

"A"   Candidates who appear, at least on paper, to have the required qualifications and experience.

"B"   Candidates who may fit but there are questions about the content and/or quality of résumé preparation. If there are sufficient "A" candidates, "B" candidates become "C" candidates.

"C"   This category is for candidates not qualified. If the advertisement was "blind" (a box number without the name of the employer or of the recruiting agency) these résumés are usually discarded.

The second task of the recruiter is to screen "A" category candidates by telephone. If there is a lack of sufficient "A" candidates, "B" candidates are included in the telephone interviews.

Candidates at this stage may be washed out of the recruiting process for a number of reasons, including the following:

- The candidate is over- or under-qualified;
- The candidate's salary range is too high or low;
- The candidate imposes a geographic limitation;
- The candidate is rude to the recruiter;
- In reviewing the résumé with the candidate, serious

questions not apparent in the résumé itself are raised about the candidate's qualifications, work history, and/or attitude.

The final task is to provide the person who makes the hiring decision (Department Manager or Supervisor) a list of suitable candidates. Then an interview is scheduled with the person who has the final hiring authority, and if all goes well, then the recruiter will conduct a reference check prior to an offer being made.

Cover Letters

The purpose of the cover letter is to communicate a specific personalized message about your value to a company. Cover letters are easy to write and they give you a competitive edge over all the other résumés. When you have a personalized cover letter it shows that you have researched the company and that extra effort is noticed by both personnel managers and people who make the hiring decision.

The general guidelines are:

1. Send the cover letter to the decision maker.
Make sure you have the correct spelling and title of the person. If you are responding to a newspaper advertisement, call the company for the information.

The call would sound something like this:
  (ad is for a senior loan-processor position, company name listed, send résumé to personnel)
  Voice: Coast Savings and Loan. Can I help you?
  You: Could I have the name of the branch manager?
  Voice: This is the corporate office. What branch did you want?

You: I don't know. I would like to speak to someone concerning the advertisement in today's paper for a loan processor. (under your breath: damn I didn't know it wasn't a branch)

Voice: Just a minute, I'll connect you.

Voice: Personnel.

You: I would like to speak to someone concerning the advertisement in today's paper for a loan processor. Could you tell me what type of advancement potential that position has?

Voice: I am not sure. Just a minute.

Voice: Loan Processing Department. This is Judy.

You: This is Nicole Ashman and I would like some information about the loan-processing position advertised. Could you tell me what types of loans this position deals with?

Voice: Primarily with new builds. We have had such an onslaught of ARM loans we can't keep up.

You: Who does this position report to?

Voice: Oh, that's Linda Hubacher. The manager.

You: Is that H-U-B-A-C-H-E-R?

Voice: Yes.

You: Thank you, Judy, for the information.

This may sound like a lot of work, but your résumé is now going to the decision maker and everyone else's is going to personnel.

2. Communicate something of special value in the opening line.

This means research, but it is that type of personalizing that gets you noticed.

Some examples:

- "Due to high interest rates, ARM loans have tripled."
- "While I worked for Pardee Construction, a builder of new homes,"

- "I understand that you have had an increase of ARM loans."

3. Describe how you can be valuable to the company.
Remember the working world operates on value, not need.
Some examples:
- "I feel my experience as liaison between buyers and lenders at Pardee Construction could be valuable in processing ARM loans."
- "My experience in new-home construction and customer-service skills will assist you in processing loans quickly and accurately."

4. Use the jargon and technology from that industry/field.
Find out from annual reports or trade journals and articles what is going on in that industry.
Some examples:
- Mortgage Banking: ARM's, Reg Z's, FHA, VA, Master Servicing.
- Training: Needs Analysis, Instructional Objectives, Performance-Based Instruction, Performance Criterion.

5. Ask for a personal meeting, otherwise known as the interview.
Some examples:
- "Could we get together next week to see if there is a mutual interest?"
- "I will be in your area on the twentieth of this month and would like to see you then if it's convenient."

If you are not willing to go through this effort then do not send a cover letter. Mass-produced or standardized cover letters are seen by the interviewer as one more piece of paper and not professional. You would be better off just sending the résumé; at least that looks good.

SAMPLE COVER LETTER

Nicole Ashman
625 Hurd Ct.
San Diego, CA, 92122
(619) 555-1212

October 15, 1988

Ms. Linda Hubacher
Manager Loan Processing
Coast Savings and Loan
11 West Market Street
La Jolla, Ca, 92037

Dear Ms. Hubacher,

I recently read in "Business Week" that due to high interest rates ARM loans have tripled. This trend has hit the new-home-mortgage market in particular. I was pleased to see a loan processor position available in your company.

I feel my experience as liaison between buyers and lenders at Pardee Construction could be valuable in processing ARM loans. My customer-service skills as a liaison will assist you in processing loans quickly and accurately and still maintain a friendly image to the public. This is always a difficult balance when the buyers are under the stress and excitement of buying a new home.

With my knowledge in these areas, I am sure that I could make a contribution to your company. I will be in your area on the twentieth of this month and would like to see you then if it's convenient.

Sincerely,

Nicole Ashman

SAMPLE COVER LETTER

October 23, 1988

Mr. Evan Lynch
General Manager
Calico Cottage Candies, Inc.
1639 Lindsey Way
St. Petersburg, Florida, 92166

Dear Mr. Lynch,

Rebecca Phillips at Wells Fargo Bank told me that Calico Cottage Candies is opening a new store in San Jose. I have dealt with your company for many years and am delighted to see that you are moving closer to my home.

As the President of the Entrepreneurs Association, I have gained extensive experience in all phases of operating a small business. I am very familiar with your product lines, as I managed the "Calico Treats" promotion last Halloween in the San Jose area.

I feel that my knowledge of small business practices, the city of San Jose, and your product line could help you get the new San Jose store off to a good start. I would like to meet with you to discuss some of my ideas on the subject. I will call you in a week to ten days to set up a meeting.

Yours truly,

Fredric A. Watson

SAMPLE AD AND COVER LETTER

MANAGEMENT TRAINER

We are a rapidly expanding wholly-owned subsidiary of a Fortune 500 financial services company, headquartered in Newport Beach, California, with 50 branches throughout the United States.

We are seeking a professional trainer with excellent standup training skills as well as design capabilities. The successful candidate will have a minimum of five years of training experience in a corporate environment and be effective in dealing with a broad range of backgrounds and personalities. A master's degree is preferred. Some travel may be required. This position reports to the Senior Vice-President of Human Resources.

We offer a competitive salary and employee benefits.

If you wish a challenging opportunity with prospects of quick advancement send your résumé in confidence with salary history to:

Wall Street Journal
Box 130
Palos Verdes, CA, 96721

We are an Equal Opportunity Employer.

Suzanne P. Knight
153 Streamwood Drive
San Diego, CA, 95062

October 8, 1988

Wall Street Journal
Box 130
Palos Verdes, CA, 96721

Dear Sir/Madam:

I am applying for your Management Trainer position advertised in the Tuesday, September 8th, Wall Street Journal.

I have worked for ten years in a multiunit company as a trainer responsible for design and implementation. In addition, my undergraduate degree is in finance. I believe this is a positive match with the requirements listed in your classified ad.

I look forward to meeting you in the near future.

Best regards,

Suzanne P. Knight

Networking

As mentioned earlier, approximately 25 percent of jobs are obtained by leads through friends and/or relatives. We recommend contacting your friends and/or relatives early in your job search to let them know you're looking, keep a record of your contacts, and regularly recontact them, about once a month. The NETWORKING WORKSHEET will help keep you organized.

The term "networking" has gained much recognition in recent years. What we are really talking about, however, is maintaining friendships, keeping visible. It's the process of letting people know who you are and what you're doing.

Gaining visibility is an ongoing lifetime project. It is a deliberate process and requires a consistent effort and commitment to be successful. Finding comfortable ways to keep in touch with people is important. A personal note, thank-you or holiday card, recognition for someone's birthday or special event goes a long way.

So instead of thinking "networking" as something else to do for your job search, think of "networking" as building and maintaining friendships—something that is pleasant and fun and an ongoing process.

The NETWORKING: PEOPLE-I-KNOW WORKSHEET will help you jog your memory to list friends, relatives, colleagues, and other professional associates that need to know about your job search.

Remember, when contacting your friends, don't put them on the spot. The phone contact is not to ask them for a job but to ask for information about the marketplace and for them to keep their "ears open" for good leads. If you aren't sure how to go about this task see the Networking: Sample Telephone Statements.

"To be what we are,
and to become what we are capable of becoming,
is the only end of life."
Robert Louis Stevenson, *Familiar Quotations*[8]

Networking: People-I-know Worksheet

Write the names of individuals in each category who live in the geographical areas you want to work in.

Former Fellow Employees:

_____

_____

_____

_____

_____

_____

College or Trade School:

_____

_____

_____

_____

Teachers/Professors:

_____

_____

_____

_____

_____

Professional Association Members:

_____

_____

_____

_____

Roommates (Past and Present):

_____

_____

_____

Clergymen:

_____

_____

_____

Friends:

People I've invited to parties:

_____

_____

_____

People who have invited me to parties:

_____

_____

_____

People who belong to same club:

_____

_____

People I play sports with:

_____

_____

_____

People who live in the same neighborhood:

_____

_____

_____

People I have dated or double-dated with:

_____

_____

_____

_____

People I have sent Christmas Cards to:

_____

_____

_____

_____

_____

_____

_____

Now start an Action Plan on how and when you will contact these people. You may find the sample worksheet on the following page useful.

Networking Worksheet

(Sample)

Name and Address of Individual and Company

	Source for Name (i.e., Directory, Personal, etc.)	Initial Contact (Date)	(✓) If Reply Rec'd	Follow-up Date	Interview Date

Contact Person: _Sally Martin_

Organization: _Imperial Bank_

Address: _318 Balboa Ave_

San Diego, Ca 92801

Telephone: _714/555-1212_

Source: _Personal_ Initial Contact: _8/16_ Follow-up: _9/16_

will locate info. on salary range for trainees in banking industry.

Contact Person: _Jeff Perkins_

Organization: _USC Placement Office_

Address: _University Park_

Los Angeles, CA 93631

Telephone: _213/555-1212_

Source: _friend_ Initial Contact: _8/20_ Reply Rec'd: _9/20_

Additional copies of this form are in Appendix C.

Networking: Sample Telephone Statements

INSTRUCTIONS:

Review the questions and statements below. Notice the request is for information—not for a job. Note the statements you would feel most comfortable using.

a. "Let me know if you hear of any job openings."

b. "Let me know if you hear of anyone that's quitting his/ her job."

c. "Let me know if you know of anyone leaving his job."

d. "Would you write me an open letter of recommendation addressed "To Whom It May Concern?""

e. "Are you anticipating any openings where you work?"

f. "Could you arrange for me to talk to your employer (or personnel director) about job opportunities in your industry?"

g. "Can I use your name as a reference when I fill out applications?"

h. "You have a lot of contacts with people and might be able to help me find leads by talking to people you know."

i. "Maybe you could help me out by asking your friends if they know of any leads for me."

j. "Would you take a few copies of my résumé and give them out to anyone you think might be interested?"

k. "You recently started working yourself and I'm wondering if you might remember any places that hire people with my skills?"

l. "I have been laid off and I have now started looking seriously for a new position."

m. "I'm looking for a job in your area."

n. "Many people hear about jobs through friends, so I wanted to let you know I am looking for a job."

o. "Do you know anyone who works at . . . ?"
    "What is their name?"
    "May I tell them you recommended that I talk with them?"
    "Can I use your name?"
    "Would you be willing to call ahead, so they will know who I am when I call?"
    "Who makes the decisions to hire . . . positions at that company?"

p. "In your opinion, what type of business opportunities do you see at your company?"

q. "What type of local trade union or organization should I join?"

r. "Have you heard of any companies that are reorganizing or that have new management?"

s. "Can you recommend an employment agency?"

t. "Have you had any experience with executive recruiters?"

u. "What do you see as my primary skills?"

v. "What should I do to improve my appearance when interviewing for a job?"

w. "There is time during the job-search process that I get pretty down. Are you willing to be one of my support persons at times like this?"

x. "Would you be willing to critique my résumé?"

y. "I need some help sharpening my interview skills. Would you be willing to role-play some practice questions?"

z. "You've been a tremendous help during my job search. Thank you."

Now rewrite, in your own words, sample questions or statements that you feel most comfortable using. This step will make sure that you come across friendly, confident, and natural. It's important to project a positive self-image, and often that is difficult while searching for a new job.

1.

2.

3.

4.

5.

6.

7.

8.

9.

10.

11.

12.

13.

14.

15.

"Whoso would be a man, must be a nonconformist."
Ralph Waldo Emerson, *Selected Writings*[9]

Before the Interview Starts

What you do in a job campaign will be less than optimally productive unless you get the job offer. The key to getting the offer is to be successful in your interviews. Be informed about potential employers, and tailor the image you project to what each firm is seeking.

Besides knowing as much as you can about yourself, you should also do some careful research on the organization with which you are interviewing. The things you should know before going to an interview are:

- What products and services does the employer provide?

- What is the company's reputation in the industry, for its products and services?

- Who are its competitors?

- What are the common industry problems?

- What are the major events/activities for this company in the last three to six months?

- What is a realistic and desired salary target? Be clear about a minimum offer.

- A list of your skills and knowledge that match the position.

- A list of three to five questions you want to know about the employer.

- A list of three ways you can make a contribution to the employer.

- Anticipate the negative aspects of your background and prepare answers.

Suggestions to finding this information:

- Go to the company before the interview and ask for:
  —recruitment brochures.
  —annual reports.
  —employee newsletter.
- Go to the library for the following references:
  —*Dun & Bradstreet Million Dollar Directory.*
  —*Klein's Directory of Directories.*
  —State Manufacturing Directory for your state.

—Standard & Poor, Register of Corporations, Directors and Executives, Vol. 1–3.
—Contacts Influential.

- Use your NETWORKING WORKSHEET and ask people you know if they have any information about that particular company.
- Go to the company at lunchtime and watch where employees go to lunch. Go to the same place and strike up a conversation. If it seems to be visited frequently by that company's employees, then talk to the waiter/waitress. Keep your ears open.
- Review the exercises in this book:
    —SKILLS-ANALYSIS WORKSHEET.
    —YOUR PREFERRED-JOB PROFILE.
    —TYPICAL-QUESTIONS-EMPLOYERS-ASK WORK-SHEET.
    —QUESTIONS-TO-ASK-DURING-AN-INTERVIEW WORKSHEET.

To have that competitive edge, enter each interview with at least a basic knowledge of the company's products, services, philosophy, and have a complete understanding of yourself.

Your Appearance

Lastly, your personal appearance takes planning also. The way you dress is the single most important nonverbal communication you can make about yourself. Not only is it important, it usually sets the tone that virtually controls the rest of the interview. The following are considered fatal attitudes about appearance:

- "If they don't like me the way I am, that's too bad."

or

- "I'll be able to dress better after the job."

or

- "This is the way their employees look."

If you find yourself identifying with the statements above, you are dead in the water before you even open your mouth in the interview. Let's take a closer look at each statement.

- "If they don't like me the way I am, that's too bad."
  This is a prime example of bad attitude.
  From an employer's point of view, who needs it?
  There is a time and place for creative expression.
  The interview isn't it.
- "I'll be able to dress better after the job."
  This is a vicious circle because finances are tight.
  Do some comparative shopping, look for sales.
  It doesn't have to cost you a fortune.
  After all, the interviewer can't see the labels, only you can.
  Remember, if you dress appropriately you'll find a job faster.
- "This is the way their employees dress."
  That may be true.
  However, the employers' expectations are what we call "Sunday Best."

So what is appropriate dress?
Dress for the position for which you are interviewing. This simply means a neat and clean appearance. For example:

- A steel mill worker:
  If normal everyday dress is levis, shirt, hard hat, and steel-toed shoes, you wouldn't go to an interview dressed in a suit. In this case, new or "dress" levis, a clean and pressed long-sleeved shirt with polished shoes is appropriate.

- A Hospital or Research worker:
  If normal dress is a uniform, then wear conservative dressy sportswear. Which means clean, pressed slacks, long-sleeved shirt, belt and hard shoes. Not tee-shirts, levis and tennis shoes.
- A middle management job:
  Men should wear a conservative suit (dark blue or gray), long-sleeved solid-color shirt, tie, shined black shoes worn with dark socks, and an attaché case.
  Women should wear a conservative skirted suit (medium-blue or gray), long-sleeved solid shirt, neutral-color pantyhose, simple pumps, and an attaché case.

Some general guidelines:

- Dress on the conservative side.
- Wear fabrics that don't wrinkle. Synthetic blends that look like wool work great. Forget cotton.
- Make sure clothes fit. Too loose and too tight are equally bad.
- Avoid wearing excessive jewelry.
- Avoid strong aftershave or perfume.
- Be sure your fingernails are properly cut and clean.
- Your clothes should be fresh, neat, and pressed.
- Your shoes should not be scuffed.

The exceptions that prove the rule of conservative dress are few and far between. High creative art and entertainment jobs are where most exceptions are found. If you don't like what we have just said, it's your choice. However, some people may be eliminated from consideration for not having a "businesslike appearance" at an interview.

If you are in doubt about your current wardrobe, there are several books available on how to dress appropriately for an interview. *Dress For Success* and *The Woman's Dress For Success*, by John T. Malloy are in paperback edition and can be found in most local bookstores.

The Interview

The interview is an exchange of information. It is a give-and-take relationship. The most important purpose of an interview is to see what type of person you are and secondly to validate information on your résumé or employment application. If you are like most people, you are pretty nervous about interviewing. This is often caused by the fact that people feel they are at the mercy of the interviewer, that they have no control. The reality of the situation is an interviewer controls the flow of the interview, but you control the content. The best way to control the content of the interview is to be prepared—and that's what we are going to do now.

Let's deal with your attitude about interviewing by looking at some common fallacies:

- The interviewer is an obstacle trying to screen you out.

  Truth: The interviewer (decision maker) wants to determine your interest in obtaining the job and what contribution or value you can bring to solve his/her problem.

- Most employers are professional (trained) interviewers.

  Truth: Most employers have NOT had training in interviewing skills. They are often just as uncomfortable as you are. The exception is if you are going through personnel (a screening interview) and/or dealing with one of the top Fortune 500 companies.

- The most skilled and experienced person gets the job.

  Truth: Employers hire people they like, who prove in the interview that they can make a contribution.

DOES AN INTERVIEW FOLLOW A PATTERN?

A typical half-hour interview consists of four segments. Interviewers' styles vary from very formal to casual, but most will begin by attempting to establish rapport. Be prepared to comment pleasantly on the weather, your hobbies, or some other seemingly unimportant topic. The interviewer is trying to put you at ease and at the same time to observe your communication skills, personal manner, and level of enthusiasm. Studies indicate that positive or negative impressions are created in the first few minutes of an interview—make that time count for you. For example:

> *Interviewer:* "Hi, Rich, sorry to keep you waiting." (make eye contact).
> *You:* (While walking into office.) "That's all right, Mr. Bleau. It's a pleasure meeting you. I've been looking forward to this interview." (in the office) "I was reading your newsletter in the lobby—it really looks quite impressive."
> *Interviewer:* "Thanks. Why don't you sit here and we can get started."
> *You:* "Sure. I've noticed that everyone here seems to enjoy plants. It sure makes the whole place pleasant."
> *Interviewer:* "Yes, I agree. Well, to start, tell me a little about yourself."

Remember, by "breaking the ice" we mean establishing some kind of psychological contact with the interviewer. To let him or her know that you are present, alive, well, and ready to begin. The key ingredients are:

- a smile.
- direct eye contact.
- the words, "Hi, I'm (first and last name)."
  "It's a pleasure to meet you."
- a firm but gentle handshake.

Next, an interviewer will usually ask questions about your background, qualifications, and career goals. Your answers should be organized and well thought-out when possible. Be informative without boasting or complaining. Make your responses positive. For instance, if asked about your greatest weakness, identify it and talk about how you are working to improve in that area. Always give enough detail to convey your point, but do not ramble. Keep in mind that your self-confidence and ability to relate to others will be measured along with the content of your answers. For example:

Interviewer: "In your opinion, what is your greatest weakness?"
You: "Sometimes my wife tells me I'm too concerned about doing a good job at work. I pay attention to details especially during month-end closing."

You will get a chance to deal with these types of questions in the Blockbuster-Interview Worksheet.

The third segment will often deal with how you might fit into the company. The interviewer will describe the organization, training programs, and career opportunities. Use this time to ask any questions you have prepared or that are stimulated by the interviewer's remarks. An interview is give-and-take, an information session for both of you. Do not be discouraged if salary and benefits are not discussed; these topics can wait for the second interview. For example:

Interviewer: "How far do you think you can go in this company? Why?"
You: "Eventually, I'd like to work my way up to being a Senior Systems Analyst. I think the environment here is conducive to the development of its employees. Your products, credibility in the marketplace, and growth potential are all excellent. I'm interested in contributing to its goals and know my efforts will be recognized."

The fourth segment of the interview is your chance to get an indication of how the interviewer feels about how you might fit into the organization. You might be asked to complete an application, speak to someone else in the company, visit the company's plant, or take a test. If an interviewer neglects to mention follow-up, ask when you can expect to hear from him or her again. If the interviewer is really impressed with you, your own selling job may conclude the interview. If not, ask for the job. Do not be afraid—you've got nothing to lose and a lot to gain. Whether you get the answer you wanted or not, always thank the interviewer for his or her time and exit gracefully. For example:

> *Interviewer:* "Well, Sally, that's all the questions that I have. Thank you for being so open and complete in the information you provided. Are there any additional questions?"
>
> *You:* "No, I think that's about it. However, I'd like to take a few seconds to sum things up. Would that be okay with you, Mr. Harrison?"
>
> *Interviewer:* "Sure, go ahead."
>
> *You:* "This has been a real opportunity to look at your company. I feel that with my abilities to organize and communicate, and being results-oriented, I would make a significant contribution. I'm very excited about this and feel confident that the match is positive. When will you be making your final decision?"
>
> *Interviewer:* "Sometime next week."
>
> *You:* "Thank you for your input, I've enjoyed this interview. (Stand and shake hands.) Hope to hear from you soon."

By "closing" the interview we mean finding an area of agreement and letting the employer know you can contribute and are interested in the job. The key ingredients are:

- A smile.
- Direct eye contact.

- The words:
  "It sounds like a great opportunity...."
  "I look forward to hearing from you...."
  "My background fits this position well...."
  "We have a good match here...."
  "I'm excited about the position...."
- A firm but gentle handshake.

The more experienced you become at interviewing, the more relaxed you will feel. Practice some mock interviews with friends or in front of a mirror. A sincere approach is always best—act naturally, but professionally.

Polishing Your Interviewing Skills

Each interview is different, but there are several basic questions every interviewer has in mind:

- What are your strongest skills and knowledge?
- How can you contribute to this company?
- What are you looking for in a job?
- What would you like to know about the company?
- How do your skills relate to the company's needs?

Good answers to these questions require preparation and poise during the interview.

As part of developing your Personal Marketing Plan, you took a long, hard look at your skills. Review the data from TAKING GOOD CARE OF YOURSELF, concentrating on where your strengths lie and what specific job-related skills you have to offer. You can also prepare for the interview by formulating answers to the TYPICAL-QUESTIONS-EMPLOY-ERS-ASK WORKSHEET. We have prepared three different categories of typical questions:

- **"Blockbuster Questions"** because they tend to take your breath away and your heart sinks when they are asked.
- The **"10-Minus"** category are for individuals with less than ten years work experience.
- The **"10-Plus"** questions are for individuals with ten years or more work experience and/or management positions.

We recommend that you formulate answers to the "Blockbuster Questions" and either the "10 + " or "10 − " category, whichever is most appropriate.

As we have said before, good preparation will pay off in two areas—the quality of your answers and your confident attitude during the interview. So let's get started!

Typical-questions-employers-ask Worksheet

BLOCKBUSTER QUESTIONS

INSTRUCTIONS:

Write down how you would answer each question. If you find a particular question difficult, ask yourself, "What does the employer really want to know?"

1. Why are you leaving (or did you leave) your current (or last) position?
HINT: Forced resignation is not as negative as Fired. Always remain positive. Never bad mouth previous employer.

2. What do you consider to be your greatest strengths and weaknesses?
HINT: Have list of three each. Refer to Skills-Analysis Worksheet. Remember make your weakness as positive as pos-

sible. It's important to have weaknesses so employer knows you're human.

3. What is unique about yourself?
HINT: Different way of asking about strengths. Use strong value statements, something you know employer is looking for.

4. How would you describe yourself? or, Tell me a little about yourself.
HINT: Very broad question. Ask for clarification or focus on professional career. Often employer uses this question to assess your communication ability so do not ramble. Be clear and concise.

5. What are your compensation requirements?
HINT: Try not to give an amount. If they insist, give a range. Do not give exact dollar amount.

6. Will you relocate? Does relocation bother you?
HINT: Do not narrow down to a specific city or state unless it is a personal requirement.

7. Are you willing to travel?
HINT: Provide a range (e.g., 10–20 percent). Not an exact number unless it's a personal requirement.

8. What interests you most/least about this position?
HINT: Relate "most" into your strongest skills. Relate "least" to a positive by associating it with a skill you are interested in learning.

9. What did you think of your last boss?
HINT: No negatives. Think real hard about a positive and say it with conviction.

10. Why should I hire you over a person with more/less experience than you?

HINT: The real issue here is how you can make a better contribution than someone else. Don't let your own bias on age, salary, etc., cloud your answer. Answer this question by reviewing your strengths that can contribute to the job.

11. Why have you been unemployed for so long?
HINT: The real question is, is there something wrong with you? Your answer should include references to just now starting to look for a job, took a vacation, etc. The employer wants to know if you're OK. If you took a long time between jobs stress the positive things you did for self-improvement.

12. What do you have to offer this company? How can you contribute?
HINT: Have list of three or four skills or knowledge.

13. Why should I hire you?
HINT: Variation of previous question.

14. What are your expectations about this job?
HINT: They are either checking to see how closely you are listening or what type of research you did prior to the interview.

15. What do you think it takes to be successful in a company like ours?
HINT: This is a variation of 'how can you contribute?' They are looking at your standards and meaningful expectations.

16. Why are you interested in this company?
HINT: Seeing if you did any research.

17. What do you do in your spare time?
HINT: Looking for active, well-rounded person. This is the time to talk about hobbies etc.

18. Please describe a situation where your work was criticized?

HINT: What is your attitude toward change? Talk about how you felt and what you did differently. Accept blame or criticism, do not point finger at someone else.

"10 MINUS" QUESTIONS

1. What do you see yourself doing five years from now?
HINT: Issue is realistic expectations.

2. What do you really want to do in life?
HINT: Issue is how happy are you.

3. Why did you choose the career that you are in?
HINT: Planned or just happened.

4. What motivates you to put forth your greatest effort?
HINT: Issue is how well do you know yourself. Also can talk about what type of environment or boss you like to work for.

5. Why did you select your college or university?
HINT: Do you plan or just let things happen?

6. How would you describe the ideal job for you?
HINT: How can you contribute to this job? This is the time to emphasize your strengths.

7. What are your hobbies?
HINT: Are you active and well rounded or lazy. If you don't have any hobbies then talk about things that interest you. Employers want well-rounded people.

8. Tell me a story.
HINT: Assessing your communication ability. Do not ramble. Use this time to talk about an important event or how you like doing or learning something. Make sure topic is non-controversial.

9. What type of boss do you prefer?
HINT: No negatives, positives only. Refer back to your worksheet.

10. Have you ever had any difficulty getting along with fellow students, workers, or bosses?
HINT: Turn any negatives into positives by admitting you learned from situations. Do not turn this into a complaining session.

11. Have you plans for further education?
HINT: How flexible are you? Are you still interested in growing? Are you willing to do things differently? The focus of this question is not just formal education.

"10 PLUS" QUESTIONS

1. What are your long-range and short-range goals and objectives? When and why did you establish these goals, and how are you working to achieve them?
HINT: How do your personal goals fit into this organization? How long will you stay?

2. How do you determine or evaluate success?
HINT: What's important to you? What are your standards? Are you self-motivated or do you have to be told you're doing a good job?

3. Describe the relationship that should exist between a supervisor and subordinate.
HINT: What working environment and values are important to you? Refer to your worksheets to answer question. This is your opportunity to describe the ideal working relationship.

4. What two or three accomplishments have given you the most satisfaction? Why?
HINT: Tie accomplishments to issues important to em-

ployer. Employers want happy, confident and positive employees.

5. In what kind of work environment are you most comfortable?
HINT: Variation of question number three.

6. How do you work under pressure?
HINT: How stable are you? How much stress, overtime and weekend work can you handle?

7. What major job-related problems have you encountered, and how did you deal with them?
HINT: How do you deal with adversity? This is the time to talk about your ability to cope and work with others.

8. What have you learned from your mistakes?
HINT: It's all right to admit to mistakes as long as you accept the blame and learn from them. Never blame others.

9. Any position has a few negatives. What would you say you liked least about your last position?
HINT: Do not bad-mouth former boss or employer. If possible, take negative and show how it doesn't apply to new employer.

10. What planning process have you found useful, and how do you go about it?
HINT: Are you organized? The employer wants to know how you communicate your activities/plans to others.

11. What have you done in the last few years about your own development?
HINT: Are you interested in growth? Are you flexible?

Some employers ask the same questions of every candidate, no matter what position he is applying for. Usually an employer looks for intensity of principles and values when asking nonwork-related questions. Remember, nothing beats proper preparation.

Questions-to-ask-during-an-interview

INSTRUCTIONS:

Review each question and select at least five (5) that are most important to you. Then rewrite the questions in your own words.

1. Why is the position open?
2. What are the best/worst parts of the job and the company?
3. What is the typical career path?
4. How do you feel about promotions from within?
5. How do you rate your competition?
6. What do you consider to be your firm's most important asset?
7. Could you tell me a little about your role with the company?
8. What are your plans for expansion?
9. What kind of people do you usually look for?
10. What do you see ahead for your company in the next five years?
11. Do you see a recession or a boom ahead for your industry as a whole?
12. What kind of staff turnover do you have?
13. Are there any major problems now or brewing in the future?
14. How is performance measured?
15. What is the manager like? (management style)
16. Who are the key people you interface with?
17. What are the unique opportunities of the job?

148

18. What type of training or orientation is provided?
19. Do you think what I've told you about myself fits what you are looking for?
20. What are the requirements for this position?
21. Is there anything else you would like to know about my background?

Save any questions about vacation, benefits, holidays, working hours, or salary until you have received an offer. It is not appropriate to initiate that type of discussion during the screening or initial interview. It gives the employer the impression that you are more interested in what they can do for you instead of what you can do for them.

1. _____
_____
_____

2. _____
_____
_____

3. _____
_____
_____

4. _____
_____
_____

5. _____
_____
_____

INTERVIEWING DO'S

1. Control the interview by answering questions with well-prepared answers and then asking the interviewer a prepared question of your own.
2. Maintain good poise, body language, and eye contact.
3. You should address the employer concern, Why should I hire you?
4. Dress the part (Sunday best).
5. Be attentive and alert.
6. Communicate your interest to the interviewer.
7. Go into the interview with the frame of mind that you are also interviewing the company.
8. Prepare and plan before all interviews.
9. Relax and keep your cool.
10. Avoid controversy.
11. Talk in positive terms, keep your doubts to yourself.
12. Enthusiasm begins with a positive attitude.
13. Be prompt or early for your interview.
14. Learn as much as you can about the interviewer's company problems, objectives, and opportunities.
15. Find out how your references will respond to a check.
16. Prepare good news for questions about your private life.
17. If a question is ambiguous ask for clarification.

INTERVIEWING DON'TS

1. Don't complain about anything. Not the weather, not your industry, not your former employer, and not your personal problems.
2. Don't talk money, if you can avoid it, until after you receive at least a tentative job offer.

3. Don't be overly personal or "buddy-buddy" with anyone in the company.

4. Don't be a name dropper.

5. Don't be late.

6. Don't act as if you know more than the interviewer.

7. Don't interrupt.

8. Don't be too quick to give an obvious answer (think it out).

9. Don't ask multiple questions.

10. Don't eat, chew, or smoke during an interview.

11. Don't make tension-causing judgments.

12. Don't worry about failure. Trust yourself to react properly.

13. Don't respond to a serious question with a flip joke.

After the Interview

You should follow up an interview with a brief thank-you letter, restating your interest in the company, your primary assets and accomplishments, and convincingly describing how you can benefit the employer. This note of appreciation for the interviewer's time is often the extra touch that secures a job offer. The follow-up letter is one more tool to put your résumé at the top of the pile. Invariably when a person receives your letter they try to match it up with the application and résumé.

It is critical that you get this letter into the mail on the day of the interview or no later than the following day. This takes discipline. If you are resisting this step, then take a hard look at your desire to represent an effective and professional image. As far as that goes, how bad do you really want to work? We know this sounds a little strong; however, the follow-up letter is the single most effective post-interview technique you can use.

The following are examples of brief thank-you letters.

SAMPLE THANK-YOU LETTER

October 30, 1988

Mr. Donald Parker
Alsado Porsche Audi
21246 68th Avenue South
Seattle, Washington, 98032

Dear Mr. Parker,

Thank you for providing the opportunity for me to learn more about Alsado Porsche Audi, and the position of Customer Service Manager.

I was interested in the position before our meeting, and I now await with great anticipation the next step in the selection process.

Sincerely,

Steve Bergsma

SAMPLE THANK-YOU LETTER

October 4, 1988

Mr. Daniel Perkins
NSK Incorporated
55 East 52nd Street
New York, New York, 10055

Dear Mr. Perkins,

Thank you for the time and courtesy you extended me during my recent interview yesterday.

After learning more about the Controller position, I am convinced that I can make an immediate contribution to NSK Incorporated due to my experience with multiunit retailers and financial background.

It's an exciting opportunity, and I look forward to hearing your decision very soon.

Best regards,

Christopher Knott

SAMPLE THANK-YOU LETTER

October 7, 1988

Mr. Ralph Kimbell
Trojan Industries Incorporated
9200 S. Dadeland Boulevard
Miami, Florida, 33152

Dear Mr. Kimbell,

I enjoyed our discussion today regarding your current opening for a Benefits Assistant. Although we agreed that my qualifications are not suited to your present needs, I want you to know that I am very impressed by the quality of work done by your company. Consequently, I do hope you will keep me in mind in the event a more suitable opening occurs.

Again, my warm thanks for your consideration. I sincerely hope we have the opportunity to meet again.

Yours truly,

Pamela Myers

In many companies, the interviewing and evaluation of all available candidates can take some time. You may be invited back for a second or third interview or have an offer extended to you, but it all takes time. Have patience.

If you do not hear in one week, take a deep breath and call the interviewer. The call should go something like this:

Secretary: Mr. Perkins's office.
You: This is Roger Davidson calling. May I speak to him please?
Secretary: I'm sorry, he's stepped away from his desk/on another line/in a meeting. May I help you?
You: Mr. Perkins and I met last week regarding the Controller position.
Secretary: One minute please.

IF INTERVIEWER CANNOT TAKE THE CALL THEN:
You: When would be a good time to call back? OR, I'll hold, please.

IF INTERVIEWER DOES TAKE THE CALL:
Interviewer: This is Dan Perkins.
You: Yes, Mr. Perkins, this is Roger Davidson. I met with you last week concerning the Controller position, and I would like to know where you are in the decision-making process.
Interviewer: It's going to take at least another week before a decision can be made.
You: Am I still a leading candidate for this position?
Interviewer: Yes, one of three.
You: That's great. I really am excited about an opportunity to work with you. Is there any additional information I could provide you that would help you make your decision?

OR:

> *Interviewer:* We had several outstanding candidates, of which you were one. However, we decided on another candidate.
> *You:* Boy, I am disappointed. That probably wasn't an easy decision. I would be interested in any helpful hints on how I could improve my interview style.

Evaluating the Potential Employer

Is this the job for me?

After the interview, most people are concerned about whether the employer will want them for the job. But there is another side to the coin—do you want that job, working for that company?

As soon as you can after the interview, while information is still fresh in your mind, do some evaluating of your prospective employer. The first worksheet, EVALUATING THE POTENTIAL EMPLOYER, helps you determine what type of information you gained from your interview.

The second worksheet, INTERVIEW ANALYSIS, lets you reflect on the interview process. This worksheet will help you learn from each interview what to do differently and possibly identify other potential leads. A supply of these forms are in Appendix C.

Evaluating-the-potential-employer Worksheet

INSTRUCTIONS:

Review each question and place a check (√) beside it if you do not know the answer.

What Do I Know About The Company?
- Is it economically stable?
- Position in the marketplace?
- What is its size?
- Primary ownership and subsidiary status?
- When was the company founded?
- What is the growth rate for the company, past and projected?
- Could you recommend their goods and services?
- Are they in demand?
- Have I read pertinent industry journals or obtained the company's annual report?

Is The Compensation Package Satisfactory?
- Fair salary offer?
- Insurance—Life and Medical?
- Profit sharing? Stock options? Retirement?
- Educational reimbursement?
- Vacation policy?
- Commissions? Bonus program?
- Relocation policy?
- Travel expense and reimbursement policy?

What Is The Opportunity For Growth At This Company?
- Monetarily:
  What is the salary-review schedule?
  Historically, what is the average rate of increase?
  Does the company promote by merit or by seniority?

- Professionally:
  Can new skills be acquired?
  Will there be new responsibilities?
  What is the visibility factor of this job?

- Career:
  Can one move up the corporate ladder?
  Is there opportunity beyond what one sees initially?
  Can I earn recognition and respect for my efforts?

Is The Style Of Doing Business Compatible With Mine?
- Management style
- Approach to planning
- Ethics

Is The Company Technologically Current?
- Is the equipment or machinery adequate to perform the task?
- What is the emphasis on research and development?

If There Is A Training/Orientation Program Involved Is It Appropriate?
- By whom would I be trained?
- What is the length of the training/orientation?
- Where will training take place?

Is The Location Of The Position Appropriate?
- If sales: territory, accounts
- Position and size of office
- Geographic location
- Convenience of getting to and from work

Do I Clearly Understand What The Job Entails?
- Can I do the job or be trained in a reasonable amount of time?
- Have I interviewed with all of the appropriate company people?

- Can I reach my goals here?
- Will the job be challenging?
- How closely does this job match my preferred-job profile?
- What skills or experience can I contribute?

How Does My Family Feel About The Job?
- What effect will this job have on my private life?
- Leisure time?
- Outside personal interest and commitments?

Any checked items that are of high priority to you should be answered positively prior to accepting the job. Make a list of these questions for the second interview or phone discussion with the potential employer.

Interview-analysis Worksheet

(Sample)

Company Name: _Shearson Lehman Mortgage Corp._

Address: _19103 MacArthur Blvd., Newport Beach, 62016_

Phone: _714/ 755 - 7400_

Name and Title of Interviewer: _Janice Morton, Recruiter_

Position Interviewed For: _Training Director_

Information Gained: (Be specific: e.g., not "good company" but "sales force expected to grow 15 percent in next two years.")

Aggressive growth projected.
Cyclical industry. Backed by financial stable parent company.
Impressive headquarters. Standard benefit package.
Entreprenurial spirit. Bonus eligible. Lateral salary but
will review in six months

Questions asked by the interviewer: _Tended to ask_
traditional, insipid questions - must be new. Kept me waiting
30 minutes.

Referrals to other employers: _None_

Successful parts of the interview: _When we covered what I've_
done for Butler Restaurants. Liked design work.

Parts which did not go well or need more work: _____
Trying to be authentic & project sincerity when responding to questions
like, "Where do you plan to be in 5 yrs?" Especially asked by 22 yr
old who has yet got an AA degree.

160

Rejection

Despite the level of job-hunting skills you possess, be prepared for rejection from the majority of positions for which you are interviewed. Even in the best of situations, you can lose more than you win. Avoid the tendency to be negatively self-critical. Rejection usually comes through a phone call or by way of a letter. You may be surprised or even hurt by this rejection, but simply "chalk it up to experience." Turn rejection into a plus by asking the interviewer how you can strengthen your next interview. A key factor will be your ability to learn from your experience and use whatever constructive feedback you receive to your advantage. If one particular interview doesn't proceed smoothly, don't waste time looking back. It's a big world, and you should immediately work at exploring other opportunities. Get in touch with your feelings by spending some time redoing the worksheets in Taking Care of Yourself. Now is a good time to keep your Personal Journal up-to-date, to help you focus on positive things. Don't forget to treat yourself to something special. Now is the time to pamper yourself. You need it and you deserve it. If you are still feeling particularly overwhelmed, go away for a few days and regroup.

One way to help keep rejection in perspective is to keep a log of each time you hear a NO. Make a game of it. Cross off one NO with every rejection. The object of this game is to cross off as many NO's as fast as you can so you can finally hear a YES. The REJECTION WORKSHEET will help you keep track of your progress.

Rejection Worksheet

INSTRUCTIONS:

Cross off a "NO" for every type of rejection you receive during your job search. If you receive a "YES" write it in big bold letters and circle it! Know for every "NO" you cross off, the closer you will be to hearing a "YES."

no no no no no no no no no no no no no no no no no no
no no no no no no no no no no no no no no no YES no no
no no no no no no no no no no no no no no no no no no
no no no no no no no no no no no no no no no no no no
no no no no no no no no no no no no no no no no no no
no YES no no no no no no no no no no no no no no no no
no no no no no no no no no no no no no no no no no no
no no no no no no no no no no no no no no no no no no
no no no no no no no no no no no no YES no no no no no
no no no no no no no no no no no no no no no no no no
no no no no no no no no no no no no no no no no no no
no no no no no no no no no no no no YES no no no no no
no no no no YES no no no no no no no no no no no no no
no no no no no no no no no no no no no no no no no no
no no no no no no no no no no no no no no no no no no
no no no no no no no no no no no YES no no no no no no
no no no no no no no no no no no no no no no no no no
no no no no no no no no no no no no YES no no no no no
no no no no no no no no no no no YES no no no no no no
no no no no no no no no no no no no no no no no no no
no no no no no no no no no no no no no no no no no no
no no no no no YES no no no no no no no no no no no no
no no

If you have followed our suggestions and have addressed your capabilities to contribute effectively to a legitimate company need, you should soon find yourself working again at a job of your own choosing.

Appendices

Appendix A: Directories

Contacts Influential: Commerce and Industry Directory.
   Lists business in particular market area by name, type of business, and key personnel. Market Research and Development Services, 321 Bush St., Ste. 203, San Francisco, CA, 94104.

The Dictionary of Occupational Titles.
   U.S. Department of Labor, U.S. Government Printing Office, Washington, DC, 20402.

Dun & Bradstreet Million Dollar Directory and ***Dun & Bradstreet Middle Market Directory.***
   A three-volume alphabetical listing of companies. It lists over 120,000 companies and includes geographic- and industrial-index listings. Dun & Bradstreet, 99 Church Street, New York, NY, 10007.

Dun & Bradstreet Reference Book of Corporate Managements.
   Lists over 3,000 companies with backgrounds of officers and directors.

Encyclopedia of Associations, Vol I, ***National Organizations.***
   Lists organizations that are in the business of giving out information.

F & S Index of Corporations and Industries.
   On a weekly basis, lists published articles by industry and by company name.

Register of manufacturers for your state or area.
   Your local librarian will help you with this one. It's great if you want to stay in your local area.

If all this information on directories and which one to go to is overwhelming you, there are two Super Directories, which list all the directories. They are:

- ***Guide to American Directories.*** B. Klein & Company, 11 Third Street, Rye, NY, 10050.

- ***Directory of Directories.*** Gale Research, Book Tower, Detroit, MI, 48226.

Besides these directories, some periodicals are worth looking through: *Business Week, Forbes, Fortune,* and the *Wall Street Journal.*

Appendix B: Recommended Reading

Adams, John. *Understanding and Managing Stress: A Book of Readings* (California: University Associates, 1980).

Andersen, Christopher, and Albert Myers. *Success Over Sixty* (New York: Summit Books, 1984).

Bolles, Richard N. *The Three Boxes of Life* (Berkeley, Ca.: Ten Speed Press, 1978).

Bolles, Richard N. *What Color Is Your Parachute?: A Practical Manual for Job-Hunters and Career Changes* (Berkeley, Ca.: Ten Speed Press, 1987).

Crystal, John C., and Richard N. Bolles. *Where Do I Go From Here with My Life?* (Berkeley, Ca.: Ten Speed Press, 1974).

Ford, George A., and Gordon L. Lippitt. *Planning Your Future: A Work for Personal Goal Setting* (California: University Associates, 1972).

Holland, John L. *Making Vocational Choices*. 2nd ed. (New Jersey: Prentice-Hall, 1985).

Jackson, Tom. *Guerrilla Tactics in the Job Market* (New York: Bantam Books, 1981).

Jackson, Tom. *The Perfect Résumé* (New York: Anchor Books, 1981).

Levering, Robert, Milton Moskowitz, and Michael Katz, *The 100 Best Companies to Work for in America* (New York: Addison-Wesley, 1987).

Molloy, John T. *Dress For Success* (New York: Warner Books, Inc., 1978).

Molloy, John T. *The Woman's Dress for Success Book* (New York: Warner Books, Inc., 1978).

Neirenberg, Gerard. *The Art of Negotiation* (New York: Simon & Schuster, 1981).

Sheehy, Gail. *Passages* (New York: E. P. Dutton & Company, 1976).

Appendix C: Worksheets

Job-search Action-plan Worksheet

DATE   ACTION

——————   ——————————————————————

——————   ——————————————————————

——————   ——————————————————————

——————   ——————————————————————

——————   ——————————————————————

——————   ——————————————————————

——————   ——————————————————————

——————   ——————————————————————

——————   ——————————————————————

——————   ——————————————————————

——————   ——————————————————————

——————   ——————————————————————

——————   ——————————————————————

——————   ——————————————————————

——————   ——————————————————————

——————   ——————————————————————

——————   ——————————————————————

——————   ——————————————————————

——————   ——————————————————————

Job-search Action-plan Worksheet

DATE	ACTION
————	——————————————————
————	——————————————————
————	——————————————————
————	——————————————————
————	——————————————————
————	——————————————————
————	——————————————————
————	——————————————————
————	——————————————————
————	——————————————————
————	——————————————————
————	——————————————————
————	——————————————————
————	——————————————————
————	——————————————————
————	——————————————————
————	——————————————————
————	——————————————————
————	——————————————————
————	——————————————————
————	——————————————————
————	——————————————————

Job-search Action-plan Worksheet

DATE	ACTION

Job-search Action-plan Worksheet

DATE	ACTION

Job-search Action-plan Worksheet

DATE   ACTION

_____ _____

_____ _____

_____ _____

_____ _____

_____ _____

_____ _____

_____ _____

_____ _____

_____ _____

_____ _____

_____ _____

_____ _____

_____ _____

_____ _____

_____ _____

_____ _____

_____ _____

_____ _____

_____ _____

_____ _____

_____ _____

Networking Worksheet

Name and Address of Individual and Company	Source for Name	Initial Contact Date	(✓) If Reply Rec'd	Follow-up Date	Interview Date
Contact Person: _____	_____	_____	_____	_____	_____
Organization: _____					
Address: _____					
_____					
Telephone: _____					
Contact Person: _____	_____	_____	_____	_____	_____
Organization: _____					
Address: _____					
_____					
Telephone: _____					

Contact Person: _____

Organization: _____

Address: _____

Telephone: _____

Contact Person: _____

Organization: _____

Address: _____

Telephone: _____

Contact Person: _____

Organization: _____

Address: _____

Telephone: _____

Networking Worksheet

Name and Address of Individual and Company	Source for Name	Initial Contact Date	(√) If Reply Rec'd	Follow-up Date	Interview Date
Contact Person: _____	_____	___	___	___	___
Organization: _____					
Address: _____					
_____					
Telephone: _____					
Contact Person: _____	_____	___	___	___	___
Organization: _____					
Address: _____					
_____					
Telephone: _____					

Contact Person: _____

Organization: _____

Address: _____

_____

Telephone: _____

Contact Person: _____

Organization: _____

Address: _____

_____

Telephone: _____

Contact Person: _____

Organization: _____

Address: _____

_____

Telephone: _____

177

Classified-ad Worksheet

Where ad listed & date: _____
Response:

     Résumé Sent: _____

     Confirmation Résumé Received: _____

     Reject Letter Received: _____

     Screening Phone Call: _____

     Interview Scheduled: _____

     Follow-Up Letter Sent: _____

     Follow-Up Phone Call: _____

     Offer Made: _____

Comments: _____

_____

_____

_____

Classified-ad Worksheet

Where ad listed & date: _____
Response:

    Résumé Sent: _____

    Confirmation Résumé Received: _____

    Reject Letter Received: _____

    Screening Phone Call: _____

    Interview Scheduled: _____

    Follow-Up Letter Sent: _____

    Follow-Up Phone Call: _____

    Offer Made: _____

Comments: _____

_____

_____

_____

Classified-ad Worksheet

Where ad listed & date: _____
Response:

    Résumé Sent: _____

    Confirmation Résumé Received: _____

    Reject Letter Received: _____

    Screening Phone Call: _____

    Interview Scheduled: _____

    Follow-Up Letter Sent: _____

    Follow-Up Phone Call: _____

    Offer Made: _____

Comments: _____

_____

_____

_____

Classified-ad Worksheet

Where ad listed & date: _____
Response:

    Résumé Sent: _____

    Confirmation Résumé Received: _____

    Reject Letter Received: _____

    Screening Phone Call: _____

    Interview Scheduled: _____

    Follow-Up Letter Sent: _____

    Follow-Up Phone Call: _____

    Offer Made: _____

Comments: _____

_____

_____

_____

Direct-company-contact Worksheet

List a Minimum of 100 Firms to Contact

Name, Address, and Phone Number of Company	Name of Person to Contact and Title	Date Contacted	Response
_____	_____	_____	_____
_____	Comments:		
_____			
_____			
_____	_____	_____	_____
_____	Comments:		
_____			
_____			
_____	_____	_____	_____
_____	Comments:		
_____			
_____			
_____	_____	_____	_____
_____	Comments:		
_____			
_____			

Direct-company-contact Worksheet

List a Minimum of 100 Firms to Contact

Name, Address, and Phone Number of Company	Name of Person to Contact and Title	Date Contacted	Response
_____	_____	_____	_____
_____	Comments:		
_____			
_____			
_____	_____	_____	_____
_____	Comments:		
_____			
_____			
_____	_____	_____	_____
_____	Comments:		
_____			
_____			
_____	_____	_____	_____
_____	Comments:		
_____			
_____			

Direct-company-contact Worksheet

List a Minimum of 100 Firms to Contact

Name, Address, and Phone Number of Company	Name of Person to Contact and Title	Date Contacted	Response
_____	_____	_____	_____
_____	Comments:		
_____			
_____			
_____	_____	_____	_____
_____	Comments:		
_____			
_____			
_____	_____	_____	_____
_____	Comments:		
_____			
_____			
_____	_____	_____	_____
_____	Comments:		
_____			
_____			

Direct-company-contact Worksheet

List a Minimum of 100 Firms to Contact

Name, Address, and Phone Number of Company	Name of Person to Contact and Title	Date Contacted	Response
_____	_____	_____	_____
_____	Comments:		
_____			
_____			
_____	_____	_____	_____
_____	Comments:		
_____			
_____			
_____	_____	_____	_____
_____	Comments:		
_____			
_____			
_____	_____	_____	_____
_____	Comments:		
_____			
_____			

Agency-contact Worksheet

Use a separate worksheet for each agency contacted, and list employers they send you to.

Agency Name, Address, Telephone Number, and contact person.

	Date Resume Mailed	Type of Response	Recommended Follow-up, i.e., Telephone Call, Visit, Etc.	Referrals
Company: _____	_____	_____	_____	_____
Address: _____				
_____	Comments:			
Telephone: _____				
_____				
Company: _____	_____	_____	_____	_____
Address: _____				
_____	Comments:			
Telephone: _____				
_____				
Company: _____	_____	_____	_____	_____
Address: _____				
_____	Comments:			
Telephone: _____				
_____				

Agency-contact Worksheet

Use a separate worksheet for each agency contacted, and list employers they send you to.

Agency Name, Address, Telephone Number, and contact person.

	Date Resume Mailed	Type of Response	Recommended Follow-up, i.e., Telephone Call, Visit, Etc.	Referrals
Company: ————	———	————	—————	———
Address: ————				
————	Comments:			
Telephone: ———				
————				
Company: ————	———	————	—————	———
Address: ————				
————	Comments:			
Telephone: ———				
————				
Company: ————	———	————	—————	———
Address: ————				
————	Comments:			
Telephone: ———				
————				

Interview-analysis Worksheet

Company Name: _____

Address: _____

Phone: _____

Name and Title of Interviewer: _____

Position Interviewed For: _____

Information Gained: (Be specific: e.g., not "good company" but "sales force expected to grow 15 percent in next two years.") _____

_____

_____

_____

_____

Questions asked by the interviewer: _____

_____

_____

Referrals to other employers: _____

_____

_____

Successful parts of the interview: _____

_____

_____

Parts which did not go well or need more work: _____

_____

_____

Interview-analysis Worksheet

Company Name: _____

Address: _____

Phone: _____

Name and Title of Interviewer: _____

Position Interviewed For: _____

Information Gained: (Be specific: e.g., not "good company" but "sales force expected to grow 15 percent in next two years.") _____

_____

_____

_____

_____

Questions asked by the interviewer: _____

_____

_____

Referrals to other employers: _____

_____

_____

Successful parts of the interview: _____

_____

_____

Parts which did not go well or need more work: _____

_____

_____

Interview-analysis Worksheet

Company Name: _____

Address: _____

Phone: _____

Name and Title of Interviewer: _____

Position Interviewed For: _____

Information Gained: (Be specific: e.g., not "good company" but "sales force expected to grow 15 percent in next two years.") _____

_____

_____

_____

_____

Questions asked by the interviewer: _____

_____

_____

Referrals to other employers: _____

_____

_____

Successful parts of the interview: _____

_____

_____

Parts which did not go well or need more work: _____

_____

_____

Interview-analysis Worksheet

Company Name: _____

Address: _____

Phone: _____

Name and Title of Interviewer: _____

Position Interviewed For: _____

Information Gained: (Be specific: e.g., not "good company" but "sales force expected to grow 15 percent in next two years.") _____

_____

_____

_____

_____

Questions asked by the interviewer: _____

_____

_____

Referrals to other employers: _____

_____

_____

Successful parts of the interview: _____

_____

_____

Parts which did not go well or need more work: _____

_____

_____

Job-search-expenses
Worksheet

INSTRUCTIONS:

On a weekly basis summarize all expenses on this form. At
tax time your job will be much easier.

Date	Item	Cost	Method of Payment

Job-search-expenses Worksheet

INSTRUCTIONS:

On a weekly basis summarize all expenses on this form. At tax time your job will be much easier.

Date	Item	Cost	Method of Payment
_____	_____	_____	_____
_____	_____	_____	_____
_____	_____	_____	_____
_____	_____	_____	_____
_____	_____	_____	_____
_____	_____	_____	_____
_____	_____	_____	_____
_____	_____	_____	_____
_____	_____	_____	_____
_____	_____	_____	_____
_____	_____	_____	_____
_____	_____	_____	_____
_____	_____	_____	_____
_____	_____	_____	_____
_____	_____	_____	_____
_____	_____	_____	_____
_____	_____	_____	_____

Notes

1. Beth Brophy et al., "You're Fired," *U.S. News & World Report* (23 March 1987) 11:50.

2. Henry David Thoreau, *Walden* (New York: New American Library, 1960), 10.

3. Employment Development Department, State of California, *Finding a New Job with the Skills You Already Have* (1981): 28.

4. Howard Rudnitsky and Jay Gissen, "Chesebrough-Ponds: The Unsung Miracle." *Forbes* (September 1981): 105.

5. Dag Hammarskjold, *Markings.* 6th ed. (New York: Ballantine Books, 1985), 3.

6. John Bartlett, *Familiar Quotations.* ed. Emily Morison Beck, 15th ed. (Boston: Little Brown, 1980), 686.

7. Sol Gordon, *The New You: A Book of Life.* (New York: Bantam Books, 1979), 10.

8. John Bartlett, *Familiar Quotations.* 15th ed. Emily Morison Beck (Boston: Little Brown, 1980), 668.

9. Ralph Waldo Emerson, *The Selected Writings of Ralph Waldo Emerson's Essays: Self-Reliance.* First Series. ed. Brooks Atkinson. (New York: Modern Library, 1940), 148.

Index

ABOUT THE AUTHORS

Karen S. Wolfer is an independent management consultant. Her clients include Motel 6, KMG Main Hurdman, Shearson Lehman Mortgage, and Burlington Northern Railroad. She also serves on the board of Multi Image Productions, Inc. Ms. Wolfer was formerly with Fotomat Corporation for 12 years, in charge of training and management development. She developed an outplacement program for Fotomat Corporation, which transitioned 800 employees during the corporation's relocation to Florida.

Richard G. Wong is Vice-President of Human Resources for American Express Travel Related Services. He has worked for fourteen years managing the human-resources function for domestic and international divisions and subsidiaries of Ralston Purina Company, TRW, Smith International, Inc., and Shearson Lehman Mortgage. He has taught for a number of years at Loyola Marymount University's Center of Industrial Relations and the University of California Extension. He coauthored "1-in-5's: Group Sensing," which was published in *Organization Development: Strategies for the Future* by the American Society of Training and Development.

ANNOUNCEMENTS

We see this workbook as a living document and encourage your comments and/or suggestions to improve it. Please mail your responses to:

Karen S. Wolfer and Richard G. Wong
c/o Katherine Schowalter
John Wiley & Sons
605 Third Avenue
New York, NY 10158